8-23-73

2

Industrial Color Technology

Industrial Color Technology

A symposium sponsored by

the Division of Industrial

and Engineering Chemistry

at the 156th Meeting of the

American Chemical Society,

Atlantic City, N. J.,

Sept. 11, 1968.

Ruth M. Johnston and Max Saltzman,

Symposium Chairmen

ADVANCES IN CHEMISTRY SERIES **107**

AMERICAN CHEMICAL SOCIETY

WASHINGTON, D. C.   1971

ADCSAJ 107 1-177 (1972)

Library of Congress Catalog Card 73-184207

ISBN 8412-0134-X

PRINTED IN THE UNITED STATES OF AMERICA

Advances in Chemistry Series

Robert F. Gould, *Editor*

FOREWORD

ADVANCES IN CHEMISTRY SERIES was founded in 1949 by the American Chemical Society as an outlet for symposia and collections of data in special areas of topical interest that could not be accommodated in the Society's journals. It provides a medium for symposia that would otherwise be fragmented, their papers distributed among several journals or not published at all. Papers are refereed critically according to ACS editorial standards and receive the careful attention and processing characteristic of ACS publications. Papers published in ADVANCES IN CHEMISTRY SERIES are original contributions not published elsewhere in whole or major part and include reports of research as well as reviews since symposia may embrace both types of presentation.

CONTENTS

PREFACE

The industrial application of color technology has reached a major crossroad. In the past decade great progress has been made by scientists in industry in applying the objective techniques of color science. Major benefits have been realized by using color measurement and colorant formulation theory, replacing the trial and error methods based on visual observation alone. The practicability of this approach has been proved, but problems still remain.

Accordingly, a special symposium was arranged to give a concise, "state of the art" summary of the application of this specialized science to industrial processing. This volume is a collection of those papers.

The first chapters discuss the basic concepts of the science of colorimetry, color measurement, color difference metrics, color appearance, and the importance of the engineering aspects of the materials involved. This introductory material is necessary for an audience which may not have been exposed to the various specialized aspects of the sciences involved. Only a few universities offer courses in the science and technology of color because the interdisciplinary nature of color science does not fit readily into their rigid curriculum. Hence, the topics presented in the first six papers were selected to provide a guide to those aspects of the science which are of the greatest practical importance in industrial processing. The practicing specialist may chafe at certain omissions and may criticize the elementary level, but it is hoped that the non-specialist will garner sufficient insight and be exposed to enough of the most important literature references to pursue the subject further.

Included in this first group of papers is the presentation on the perception of color. This fascinatingly beautiful lecture is reproduced here with illustrations which, to as great an extent as is possible in two dimension, serve to emphasize the complexity of the human visual process. It is a distinct privilege to be able to present this classical lecture in printed form. It is hoped that it will be a constant reminder of the limitations of a purely technical approach to a psychophysiological phenomenon.

The second part of the program begins with a paper on colorant formulation theory. This is followed by papers presented by practicing color scientists in various representative industries. It was impossible to include papers from all of the colorant-using industries, but a sufficient number are included so that the reader can form an impression about the extent to which the tools and techniques of color science have been applied.

It is an honor to have Dr. Wallace Brode, former president of both the American Chemical Society and of the Optical Society of America, provide the introductory lecture on the interdisciplinary character of color science. It is largely through his efforts when he was president that the ACS has become a member body of the Inter-Society Color Council.

RUTH M. JOHNSTON

Newburgh, N. Y.
May 1970

The Interdisciplinary Character of Color Science

WALLACE R. BRODE

Washington, D. C.

The collected papers presented at the symposium on "Industrial Color Technology," held at the 156th meeting of the American Chemical Society at Atlantic City (September 1968) provide an interesting and instructive aspect of an interdisciplinary subject within various industrial and chemical areas.

Chemical spectroscopy has thrived and expanded in the past third of a century since I published "Chemical Spectroscopy," and chemists have taken a leading role in the wide application of spectrochemical analysis in both qualitative and quantitative areas. The identification of elements, compounds, structural forms, functional groupings, and complex molecules has been facilitated by these methods. However, a separate area of physical science known as *color* involves a quite different technological approach.

Color is a visual sensation influenced by physiological, psychological, and physical factors and is developed in the eye through receptors which involve phototropic chemical reactions and nerve transmission of stimulus. Color is appreciated and enjoyed by both scientists and non-scientists; combinations of color may be beautiful and pleasing to some although to others they may be irritating. Color plays a most important part in industry as well as art. The fact that scientific deductions can be made from color emphasizes the importance of this physical property. Scientists in various disciplines may draw quite different information from colors, and hence a variety of methods of measurement and description have been developed. For some, color is absorbed radiant energy indicative of chromophoric or resonance structures; for others it is emitted or reflected light, and the chief interest is in the transmitted light rather than the absorbed.

Because of the unusual sensitivity character of the eye as an instrument or radiant energy receptor in the evaluation and recognition of color, and the large number of these "instruments" in the hands of non-scientific, albeit sophisticated operators and observers, who have developed sensitivity to color shades and combinations of color, it is highly desirable to separate color description from a more scientific spectrophotometric description in which the receptor, as a photocell or physical receiver, can be instrumented to qualitative and quantitative response over a wavelength range without physiological or psychological effects. The major industries of color photography, color printing, color television, and many other areas depend on the integrating ability of the eye to accept simulation of colors by mixing or chemical chromophores or illuminants.

It has become increasingly important to be able to define colors by terms which will permit commercial and easily comprehended definition with an accuracy which permits satisfactory color control and matching in industrial and analytical operations as well as producing satisfactory materials for public acceptance.

Symposia in the Division of Industrial and Engineering Chemistry have, on various occasions, served as the incentive for a new approach to chemistry. A symposium in this Division on dyes, held in September 1918 resulted in the organization of a Section on Dye Chemistry, which held its first meeting the next year. The years that followed were critical in the development of the emerging American dye industry. The Section became a separate Division of the Society in 1920 and continued as such until 1935 when the Dye Division merged, at its own request with the Division of Organic Chemistry. In a sense this was a move toward chemical composition and synthesis, for the areas of application, description, and classification were being at least partially covered by the Inter-Society Color Council and the American Association of Textile Chemists and Colorists.

An interdisciplinary area which appeared to be essential to almost all areas of science with respect to color was that of description of color. To cover this need to provide a common language of description the Inter-Society Color Council (ISCC) has had a most important position. The ISCC has been a major factor in the establishment of illuminant and color standards through the International Commission on Illumination (usually referred to in this volume as "CIE" (from the French terminology Commission International de l 'Eclairage) rather than "ICI" which is easily confused with a major chemical producer of dyes and pigments.

The need for a common language in describing color in the many scientific and industrial areas in which it becomes a descriptive factor resulted in the combination of some 20 scientific and engineering societies' joining together to form an Inter-Society Color Council (ISCC) in 1931. Today this group includes more than 30 societies with groups which are interested in oils, ceramics, psychology, architecture, optics, illumination, paints, pharmacy, dyes, textiles, photography, television, and many other areas in which chemistry is involved with color. However in 1950 M. G. Mellon comments in his "Analytical Absorption Spectroscopy" that "Curiously, the American Chemical Society has never cooperated (directly with the ISCC) although hundreds of its members are engaged in work involving such (color) items."

The interest evidenced by this symposium on Industrial Color Technology at the Division of Industrial and Engineering Chemistry program and as published in this volume, resulted in inquiry being made to this and other potentially interested Divisions of the Society as to our more formal support to the ISCC. As an accomplishment during my term of office as President of the American Chemical Society I was pleased to recommend that the ACS become one of the cooperating societies to the Inter-Society Color Council and to note that this action was approved by the Board of Directors in its September 1969 meeting.

Interested Divisions of the Society, including of course the Division of Industrial and Engineering Chemistry, have been asked to recommend members for appointment by the Society to serve as our representatives on the Inter-Society Color Council. It should be noted that the current Secretary and former President of the Inter-Society Color Council is Fred W. Billmeyer, Jr. who has long been an active member and councilor of the ACS and is professor of chemistry at Rensselear Polytechnic Institute as well as one of the participants and authors in this symposium volume.

Recognition should be made to Ruth M. Johnston who served as chairman of the planning committee of this symposium. Miss Johnston together with Max Saltzman and those whose papers appear in this volume formed the committee for this symposium. The over-capacity crowd which attended the symposium was a distinct compliment to the program and the importance of the subject to the society members.

2

What is Color?

An Introduction to Colorimetry

RUTH M. JOHNSTON

Kollmorgen Corp., Newburgh, N. Y. 12550

The three-dimensional nature of the color response is illustrated by the Munsell system of color notation. The CIE system of notation is based on physical measurements and forms the basis for the science of colorimetry. It takes into account the properties of the stimulus in terms of the product of the illuminant and object spectral distributions and of the spectral response characteristics of a standard observer. It was established by the International Commission on Illumination and is used universally to describe color. The science of colorimetry is limited in that "color measurements" are relative only, differences in other appearance attributes such as size, texture, glossiness, etc., are not accounted for, and differences in spectral distribution of the stimulus leads to problems of metamerism. When applied with full awareness of these limitations, colorimetry is a very useful tool.

The term "colorimetry" as used in this volume is defined as the measurement of color; thus it is the science of measuring "what we see." This use of the term "colorimetry" needs to be distinguished from the analytical chemists' use of the word. To the chemist, colorimetry generally indicates the method of relating absorption in the visible spectrum to the concentration of a substance. Likewise the instruments used for these two purposes, both called colorimeters, perform two distinctly different functions. The chemist's instrument should more properly be called a color comparator (or spectrophotometer or filter photometer if appropriate). Confusion is avoided if the term colorimeter is applied only to instruments used to measure the properties of the object which are then related to the visual sensation of color and if the term colorimetry is applied only to the numerical description determined from such measurements.

The chapters in this volume describe applications which utilize the selective spectral absorption of light as an analytical tool, but a spectrophotometric curve is not a description of color in the sense that it relates to only one aspect of the stimulus for the color response.

What then, is color? Is it sensation or perception, substance or illusion?

The Committee on Colorimetry of the Optical Society of America has defined color as consisting "of the characteristics of light other than spatial and temporal inhomogeneities, light being that aspect of radiant energy of which a human observer is aware through the visual sensations which arise from the stimulation of the retina of the eye (4). Color thus defined is psychophysical—a psychological response to a physical stimulus. It is in this sense that color is used in the subsequent remarks.

Color can mean different things to different people. To the chemist it may be a compound, a dye, or a pigment; to the physicist it may be the spectrophotometric curve of a material or of a light source; to the physiologist it may be the measurable electrical activity in the nerves that lead from the eyes; to the artist it may be an emotion; to the psychologist it may be the complex of stimulus and response mechanisms resulting in perception; to the ordinary "layman" observer, it may mean a variety of things, depending on the context in which the word is being used, although more often than not it refers to the color of an object.

In the practical world of commerce, we are most often concerned with color in this latter sense—that is, in the sense of object color. The ordinary person is concerned with the color of something as he perceives it. This perception in the complex multicolored world confounds the problems of color "pure and simple," as defined by the OSA Committee, with temporal aspects, with spatial or appearance aspects, with surround and adaptation, as well as with the individual factors of past experience and memory, attitude, and individual visual response characteristics. All of these other factors which affect the individual perceptions of color cannot be ignored, and it is important to remember this. However, in order to study color in the limiting comparative sense, where all other factors are controlled, the basic attributes common to all perceived colors can be isolated. When all other elements of the viewing situation are identical, the observed differences in color between two objects can be described as differences in hue—*i.e.,* one is greener or yellower or redder than the other—and/or differences in saturation—*i.e.,* one is grayer or contains less pure color than the other—and/or differences in brightness —*i.e.,* one is lighter or darker than the other.

The Munsell System

A method of describing color based on these psychological dimensions of hue, saturation, and lightness was originated by an artist, Albert H. Munsell, who published the first description of the notation he derived in 1905 (9). This Munsell system of color notation consists of a hue circle made up of five principal hues—red, yellow, green, blue, and purple —and five intermediate hues—yellow-red, green-yellow, blue-green, purple-blue, and red-purple. Each of the 10 hues is divided into 10 steps, plus any fractional quantities necessary; at the center of the hue circle is the gray pole, varying in lightness from black at the bottom with a value of 0 to white at the top with a value of 10. This lightness dimension is called the value. From the gray pole, the colors increase in saturation as the radius of the hue circle increases, so that the most saturated colors occur at the periphery. The saturation scale is called the chroma scale. It too was given a numerical rating from 0 for the neutrals to the most saturated colors, which occur at chroma 14 for nonfluorescent red and yellow paints. The scheme of this system is illustrated in Figure 1. A typical Munsell notation consists of a number-letter combination to describe the hue—e.g., 2.5 RP, for red-purple, a value description from 0 to 10—e.g., 3.87 for a moderately dark color, and a chroma designation such as 4.23 describing the color as of medium saturation. The chroma notation is separated from the value notation by a slash. The general form is hue, value/chroma such as 2.5 RP 3.87/4.2.

The Munsell System has now been redefined in keeping more closely with his original concepts and is called the Munsell Renotation System (11). A representation of the system consisting of small painted chips of about 1500 colors systematically sampling Munsell spacing of colors is available as the "Munsell Book of Color" (10).

The CIE System

Such collections of material representations of a system do not, however, suffice as basic standards of colorimetry. A method which does not rely on impermanent materials is required. In classical psychophysics, sensations are quantified in terms of the magnitudes of the stimulus and of the response. The stimulus for the sensation of color is the light reaching the receptors in the eye. This light may come to the eye directly from a luminous body, but more probably the light from a luminous source is modified by an obejct before reaching the eye. The nature of the light which finally stimulates the photoreceptors in the eye can be described in terms of its spectral distribution. Thus, if the spectral distribution of the light emitted by the light source is known and if the reflectance (or transmittance) of the object in terms of its relative spec-

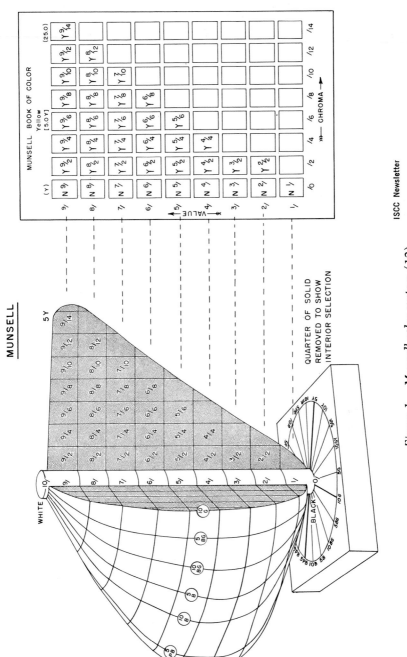

Figure 1. Munsell color system (12)

tral reflectance (or transmittance), is also known, the spectral composition of the light reaching the eye from the object illuminated by the light source can be computed. This can be done by calculating the relative amounts of the different wavelengths of light present in the source which are reflected (or transmitted) by the object. If the energy of the light source and the fractional reflectance from the object are designated as E and R respectively, this operation can be written as ER at each wavelength, λ.

An attempt to describe the nature of the response in the eye is more complex. Two principles are basic: The Young-Helmholz concept that all colors can be matched by using appropriate amounts of three primary lights (7, 15), the only restriction on the primaries being that no one of them may be matched by mixtures of the other two—and Grassman's Laws of Additive Color Mixture (6). Additive color mixture results when lights from different sources are combined—that is "added together"—to stimulate the same area of the retina. There are three methods by which additive mixing may occur: (1) spatial—e.g., illuminating a given area by means of lights from differently colored sources; (2) temporal averaging—e.g., rapidly rotating a disc made up of different colors, and (3) spatial averaging, where the stimulus is made up of areas of different color too small to be resolved as individual areas, the principle on which commercial color TV is based. Subtractive color mixture results when a material which absorbs light is placed between the observer and the source, and in the simplest case it is defined by the Beer-Bouguer Laws. This substraction of lights in the stimulus, or additivity of absorption (and/or scattering), applies to each wavelength individually.

However, Grassman's Third Law states that two stimuli which evoke the same color response will produce identical effects in additive mixture regardless of their spectral composition and that if two stimuli which evoke the same color are added to or subtracted from two other stimuli which also produce matching colors, the resulting additive synthesis will produce a color match, regardless of spectral distribution. Likewise, if the intensity of the pairs is changed by the same ratio, the colors will still match, over the range of photopic—i.e., daylight vision. Thus, additive color mixture does not apply to individual wavelengths only but relates the mixtures of stimuli or integrated spectral distributions. The science of colorimetry is based on the Young-Helmholz concept of the trichromacy of vision and on Grassman's laws of additive color mixture. With these basic principles, the nature of the observer can be defined in terms of the amounts of three primary lights necessary to mix additively so that a color match is achieved for light of each wavelength in the visible spectrum.

There is no unique set of primaries. However, regardless of the actual primaries used it is always necessary to use negative amounts of some of the primaries to match all of the wavelengths of the spectrum. Thus if the primaries selected are a red, a green, and a violet, a negative amount of the red is required to match the blue of 500 nm. To avoid using negative amounts the primaries can be transformed mathematically so that mixtures of all real colors may be represented within a triangle of positive mixtures. While the transformed primaries then become unreal, this in no way alters their validity according to Grassman's laws. The amounts of each primary required to match each wavelength are called the observer color matching functions. The definition of the observer color matching functions consists of three primary quantities for each single wavelength. The sensation resulting when this defined observer views a color of known spectral reflectance (or transmittance) in a light source of defined spectral distribution can be described in terms of the integrated products of these three quantities.

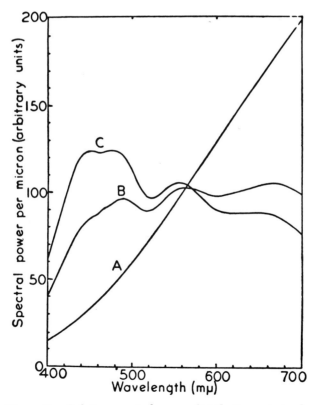

Figure 2.   *Relative spectral power distributions of stand-*
ard CIE illuminants

The need to describe the color of objects by this means becomes laborious if the distribution of the light source as well as the color matching functions for each observer must be measured individually. Hence the International Commission on Illumination in 1931 defined the spectral power distribution of three standard illuminants, illustrated in Figure 2, and established the spectral color matching functions of a standard observer, illustrated in Figure 3 (8). (The International Commission on Illumination is abbreviated CIE for Commission Internationale de l'Eclairage. In older publications the abbreviation ICI may be used.) The standard observer functions are the transformed averages of a number of observers of normal color vision when matching the halves of a field of vision subtending an angle of 2° from the normal. The observer color matching functions are designated by $\bar{x}(\lambda)$, $\bar{y}(\lambda)$, and $\bar{z}(\lambda)$ for red, green, and blue respectively. The illuminants defined represent incandescent light (A), sunlight (B), and daylight (C). Their correlated color temperatures are 2856°, 4874°, and 6774°K, respectively.

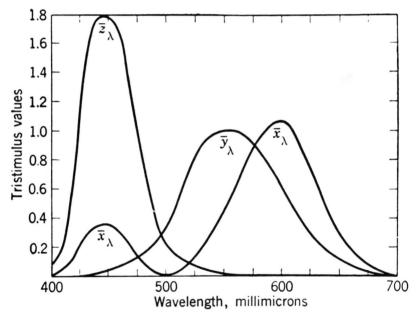

Figure 3.   *1931 CIE standard observer color matching functions (2° field)*

The integrated products of the reflectance-illuminant-observer magnitudes are called the tristimulus values, X for the red primary, Y for the green primary, and Z for the blue:

$$X = k \int R(\lambda)E(\lambda)\bar{x}(\lambda)d\lambda \qquad Y = k \int R(\lambda)E(\lambda)\bar{y}(\lambda)d\lambda$$

$$Z = k \int R(\lambda)E(\lambda)\bar{z}(\lambda)d\lambda$$

where $d\lambda$ describes the wavelength interval used in the calculation, and k is a normalizing factor.

When the transformations were made of the actual primaries used, a further important definition was made. The green or Y primary was defined to be the same as the photopic luminous efficiency function, $V(\lambda)$—*i.e.*, the spectral curve for luminosity or brightness response. Brightness response is an "achromatic" dimension in the sense that this response is not associated solely with the color response but depends only on the relative amount of light in the stimulus. The photosensitive elements of night vision (or scotopic vision) are the rods located in the peripheral region of the retina. The photochemical absorber responsible for their photosensitivity is rhodopsin which exhibits an absorption curve almost identical to the luminosity curve measured by psychophysical methods with a maximum at about 505 nm (*14*). The photosensitive elements of daylight or photopic vision are the cones. The absorption curve of one of the types of the cones concentrated in the foveal region exhibits a similar absorption maximum to the luminous efficiency curve measured for photopic vision and has a maximum at about 555 nm. Difference spectra for three types of cones have been measured (*13*).

If each of the tristimulus values is divided by the sum of the three, the fraction of the color which is attributable to each primary is obtained. Because the sum of these fractions is 1.000, two are sufficient to describe the "chromaticity" or relative contribution of each primary. These fractions are called chromaticity coordinates and are designated by x, y, z.

$$x = \frac{X}{X + Y + Z} \quad y = \frac{Y}{X + Y + Z} \quad z = \frac{Z}{X + Y + Z}$$

Any two, almost always x and y, may be plotted in rectangular coordinates for comparison. If the spectrum colors are plotted in this way, the limit locus for colors is described, with all colors falling inside these limits. Such a diagram represents the chromaticities of the additive mixture of lights. If monochromatic lights of two different wavelengths are mixed additively, the chromaticity of the resultant mixture will lie between the two chromaticities and on the straight line connecting them. If the mixture of two monochromatic lights results in white or nonchromatic light, the lights are said to be complementary. If object colors are viewed under a particular light source, the chromaticity for that light source is described as the zero point.

Advantage is taken of these properties of the system to describe the nonspectral colors which are mixtures of the short wavelength violet and long wavelength red—*i.e.*, the purples. Because all mixtures of three lights fall in a triangle formed by connecting all adjacent chromaticities with straight lines, all mixtures of the illuminant and short wavelength violet and long wavelength red must fall within the area bounded by the lines connecting the illuminant zero color with each end of the spectrum locus and the two ends of the spectrum locus with each other. If a line drawn from the illuminant chromaticity to the chromaticity point for a particular color is extended to the spectrum locus, the point of intersection on this spectrum locus describes the dominant wavelength of the color. The nonspectral purple colors are designated in terms of the dominant wavelength of the greens to which they are complementary. The dominant wavelength is similar to a description of the hue in psychological terms. The percentage of the distance of the locus for a particular color from the zero color compared with the total distance from zero color to the spectrum locus of the same dominant wavelength is called the excitation purity and corresponds roughly to the psychological dimension of satura-

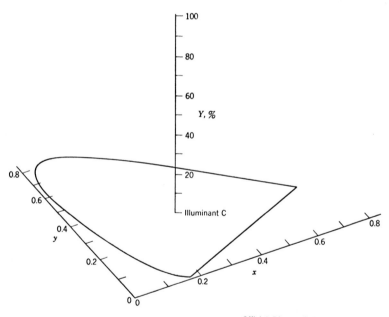

Official Digest, Federation of Societies for Paint Technology

Figure 4. CIE chromaticity diagram for illuminant C showing the third dimension, the luminance, perpendicular to the chromaticity plane
(1)

tion. The third dimension, the brightness, or Y in CIE terms, is perpendicular to the plane of the chromaticity diagram, as illustrated in Figure 4 for illuminant C. Figure 5 shows the chromaticity diagram for illuminant C with reference lines of dominant wavelength and excitation purity.

In the CIE system of colorimetry, then, the tristimulus values X, Y, and Z, are used to describe the simple color sensation. Alternate and

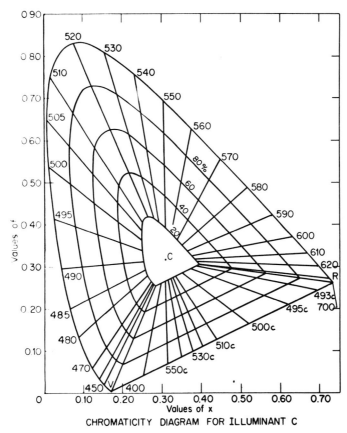

CHROMATICITY DIAGRAM FOR ILLUMINANT C

*Figure 5.   CIE chromaticity diagram for illuminant C show-
ing dominant wavelength lines and lines of equal excitation
purity at 20% intervals*

useful descriptions derived from these include the chromaticity coordinates x, y, combined with the luminous reflectance (or transmittance) Y,
or the monochromatic notation, made up of the dominant wavelength
and percent excitation purity, in combination with the luminous reflectance (or transmittance) Y. By convention in the United States, illuminant C, daylight, is used for the computation, and the 2° field data for
the 1931 observer is implied, although the CIE has now defined a 10°
field observer (1964) (2). Supplementary illuminants have also been
recommended by the CIE in 1965. These new illuminants approach more
closely the spectral energy distribution of daylight and are defined for
wavelengths 300–830 nm, allowing for use with fluorescent colors.

   This standardized system for colorimetry created by the International
Commission on Illumination is used throughout the world to describe
color. The use of this system is not limited to the description of object

colors. The color of light sources can be described by setting the reflectance equal to 1.000 at all wavelengths. When the illuminant and reflectance of object colors are defined, they can be used to describe differences in observers.

Limitations of Colorimetry

The science of colorimetry is not intended to be a theory of color vision—the science of "how we see." Vision is an extremely complex phenomenon. The trichromacy of color vision is substantiated by the data of the color mixture experiments on which the science of tristimulus colorimetry is based. However, such data do not explain the physiological and psychological mechanisms that occur. (A useful recent reference on the mechanism of vision and visual perception is the book edited by Graham (5).

The great value of the science of tristmulus colorimetry lies in its usefulness in describing the relationship of colors. Thus, there is no "absolute" color description—the notations determined by the computational procedures outlined above depend on the method by which the spectral data are obtained as well as on the computational procedures used and on the relationships of these factors to the nature of the samples that are being compared. Tristimulus values determined from measurements made on different spectrophotometers may or may not agree with one another depending on the nature of the samples, the particular instruments involved, and the wavelength intervals used in the integration. However, the differences between two similar samples, even if determined by different procedures, may not be as different as the absolute values would be. In general, one can define the probability that such measured differences will agree when determined on different instruments in terms of the nature of the samples being measured. If they are similar in appearance—i.e., if they have the same texture, gloss, etc.; and if they have similar spectral curve shapes, the chances are better that the measured differences between them will agree if measured on different instruments than if there are appearance or spectral differences between the samples being compared. The absolute measurements will not necessarily agree, however. When differences in energy distribution of the stimulus exist or when there are differences in any aspect of the appearance between two stimuli, the simple science of tristimulus colorimetry must be used with care.

Metamerism

When two stimuli consisting of different spectral distributions evoke identical color responses, they are called metamers, and the state of limited or conditional identity is called metamerism (3). The simple term "metameric match" is, therefore, used frequently to describe a pair of materials or objects with different spectral reflectance or transmittance curves. However, light sources can be metameric also—*i.e.*, two lights can appear to be the same although, in reality, they consist of different spectral distributions. The term "observer metamerism" can be used to describe a pair of observers with different spectral response characteristics. The term "geometric metamerism" has been used to refer to the state where two colors will appear to be identical under one set of illumination and viewing conditions but will be different if the geometrical conditions of observation, visual or instrumental, are changed, although more specific nomenclature for this phenomenon is being considered. According to this newly proposed nomenclature, a single specimen which changes color when the illumination or viewing angle is changed is called goniochromatic, a pair of specimens which change color with illumination or viewing angle in the same way is called gonioisochromatic, and a pair which changes color differently with illumination or viewing angle is called goniometachromatic. The aspect of colorimetry relating to such angular changes in color is then called goniocolorimetry.

The problems arising from these various kinds of metamerism cause many of the difficulties in industrial color matching. Instrument metamerism refers to instruments used for measuring color; computation metamerism is used in connection with the wavelength interval used in the integration. These adjective modifiers for the state of conditional identity known as metamerism emphasize the fundamental nature of colorimetry as a comparative science only. Hence, the science of colorimetry must be used only with the full knowledge of its basic limitations. Properly used, colorimetry constitutes a powerful tool for attacking the problems of industrial color formulation and color description because it allows for the objective treatment of the subjective appearance attribute of the color.

Literature Cited

(1) Billmeyer, F. W., Jr., *Offic. Digest, Federation Soc. Paint Technol.* **1963,** 219, 35.
(2) *CIE Proc. 1963, Vienna* **1964.**
(3) *Color Eng.* **1967,** 5 (3).
(4) Committee on Colorimetry, "The Science of Color," Crowell Co., New York, 1953.
(5) Graham, C. H., Ed., "Vision and Visual Perception," Wiley, New York, 1965.
(6) Grassman, H., *Ann. Phys. Chem.* **1853,** 89, 69.
(7) Helmholtz, H. von, "Handbuch der Physiologischen Optik," 2nd ed., Voss, Hamburg, 1896.
(8) *Intern. Comm. Illumination, Proc., 8th, Cambridge,* **1931.**
(9) Munsell, A. H., "A Color Notation," Ellis, Boston, 1905.

(10) "Munsell Book of Color," Munsell Color Co., Baltimore, 1929-1968.
(11) Newhall, S. M., Nickerson, D., Judd, D. B., *J. Opt. Soc. Am.* **1943**, 33, 385.
(12) Nickerson, D., *ISCC Newsletter* **1961**, No. 156.
(13) Rushton, W. A. H., *New Scientist* **1961**, 235, 374.
(14) Wald, G., Brown, P. K., *Science* **1964**, 144, 45.
(15) Young, T., "Lectures in Natural Philosophy," Vol. II, pp. 613–32, Savage, 1807.

RECEIVED October 10, 1969.

Color as an Aspect of Appearance

ROBERT S. FOSTER

The Borden Chemical Co., Columbus Coated Fabrics Division,
1280 North Grant Ave., Columbus, Ohio

Many factors not described by colorimetry combine to alter what is seen as color. Thus, the human eye remains the most important link in the color-matching process. Among the factors affecting light falling on a colored sample are surface characteristics, orientation effects in any of the layers of the sample, and adsorption or scattering effects of the colorants in these layers. Much remains to be done in studying and controlling these factors.

Colorimetric specifications are only under rare circumstances perceived color specifications. The human eye must still remain the most important link in the color-matching process since many factors not described by colorimetry as we know and use it today combine to alter what we see as color. Although colorimetry is a valuable tool, as indicated elsewhere in this volume, it is necessary to point out what factors in addition to colorimeter readings must be considered when evaluating a color.

In this discussion of visual effects, physiological effects such as simultaneous contrast and adaptation are not included; however, their significance should not be minimized. Knowledge of them is extremely valuable to the working color technologist, especially when working with designers attempting to create certain effects. For example, color shifts to compensate for simultaneous contrast sometimes are necessary to get the proper effect in a wallcovering print. A designer may be trying to get the effect of smoke in a vinyl handbag; viewing mode differences make this impossible (4).

Of course, there is little difference between the physiological effects and the visual phenomena we want to review. Perhaps the visual effects can best be described in terms of a match in which agreement between visual and colorimetric evaluation only occurs under closely specified conditions—in other words, a conditional match. In view of this, let us consider some of the colorimetric and visual problems occurring with the everyday matching of paint, plastics, and textiles.

Surface Reflectance

Colorimetry in practice assumes a simplified situation. A beam of light falls on a colored object, enters, is absorbed selectively, and is scattered. The remainder exits, is collected, and its spectral distribution measured. This spectral distribution is analyzed either mathematically or with optical filters to give numbers corresponding to a proportion of three primaries under standard conditions. If the numbers coincide for two samples, we have a match. In real life, this is not the case; many things can happen to the beam of light to modify and alter the numbers and/or visual appearance.

These effects are completely apart from those characteristic of the measuring instrument itself. A light beam passes from a medium of one refractive index into another, and the change in the speed of light introduces a small amount of reflectance at the surface. This amounts to about 4% of the incident radiation in most common colored media. Also, the light emerging from the interior of the medium usually undergoes an internal surface reflection. Estimates of this internal reflection are about 40% in plastics, for example (6).

The effect of a bright, mirror-like sample surface on its color is relatively easy to predict since it approaches the hypothetical, simplified model. The surface reflected light of essentially the same color as the incident radiation is reflected at an angle equal to the incident angle. This specular reflection can be eliminated either in visual or instrumental examination, unless we have the special situation of diffuse illumination.

When the surface has a structure or pattern, however, many things affecting the visual or measured appearance can occur. It may seem that this is a well-known effect, but consider Dr. Judd's postscript to the ISCC Committee 12 report on studies of illuminating and viewing conditions: "the importance of angular conditions in colorimetry tends to be forgotten, and it deserves to be continually called to our attention" (3). Many people involved with color regularly do not seem to be fully aware of the phenomenon. Often color technologists must stop and demonstrate the modifying effect of surface on a color match to such people as production supervisors, color stylists, and quality control workers.

The seemingly small proportion of incident light reflected from a surface is distributed in patterns depending on its structure and thus is included in the total evaluation of the color appearance. The structure can be a microstructure or a gloss, resulting either from the properties or pigmentation of the medium or a flatting coat. It can also be a macrostructure, decorative embossing, or texturized fabric. It is often difficult to determine which factor, micro- or macro-structure, is responsible for the particular effect observed. A bright-luster, deep-textured sample as opposed to a dull-luster, shallow-textured sample may, under some circumstances, give similar effects, thus affording a multitude of "handles" on the appearance, perhaps too many.

The effect of surface reflectance varies greatly in the different portions of color space. The amount of surface reflectance does not change with value and varies only very slightly with hue and chroma. The ratio of surface reflectance to body reflectance increases, however, with decreasing total reflectance; therefore, we can expect our greatest changes at the lower reflection levels. In general, the effect is one of graying or desaturation, this effect increasing with decreased value or increased chroma. Another effect not readily recognized is the hue shift introduced by surface reflectance. Samples of high chroma which have as part of their reflectance curves a large wavelength range of low reflectance (such as reds) exhibit this effect to a greater degree. This effect has caused more problems in practice perhaps than the lightening and graying effect. It is difficult, but necessary, to explain many times that an off-shade production sample does not necessarily call for hue correction but may only require a luster change.

One further complication is the drastic change of these effects with illumination geometry. At some angles of view or of illumination the effects may completely disappear; at others they may be strongly enhanced. Johnston has measured some of these effects and describes an "isochromatic angle" as that angle of view at which geometrically conditioned matches hold (2).

Oriented surface textures present some interesting problems also. For design or utilitarian purposes, surface reflection may be directed preferentially. An example of this is a projection screen with its extremely bright appearance concentrated on normal illumination and viewing.

Effect of Colorants

Many colored items incorporate transparent or translucent thin layers which carry colorants or diffusing and reflecting materials. These layers may be used to give mechanical protection to the item or create certain visual effects. Many of the metallic coatings used on plastics, such as automobile upholstery, fall into this category. Heavy transparent topcoatings, clear or colored, introduce variations of a visual nature since they partially alter the viewing mode. Some of the currently popular handbag and shoe materials utilize this technique to give a visual effect that is impossible to duplicate in a surface color. The angle of view also produces an appearance variable because of the changing path lengths through the top coating as the sample is turned.

This angular effect experienced with a colored top coating produces another commercially important phenomenon. It is a common practice in many industries to add lightly tinted top coats to correct off-color material. Since the perceived effect here again changes with viewing angle, an exact match is not possible between top-coated material and body colored material. The color differences admittedly are small but within the range of commercial importance. This practice of color correction by top coating is especially troublesome when it has been applied to material which is to be used as a standard for subsequent production.

Diffusing or reflecting materials are used in top coatings to give decorative effects. Pearlescent additives, consisting of flat reflecting plates, mask the base color with a specular type reflection at normal or near normal viewing angles. Newer pearlescents may also modify the color of the reflected light by interference. Viewing at an oblique angle will show the base color perhaps modified with a grayish white. Metallic flakes are used in a similar application, as indicated later.

Many directional effects can be introduced by the properties, distribution, and concentration of coloring materials within the body of the colored medium. Certain colorants have shaped particles which tend to orient during processing or application. Acicular iron oxides are particularly troublesome in this respect (1). Extreme color differences may be observed as a sample containing pigmentary iron oxide is viewed at different angles on the horizontal plane. This effect is particularly difficult to control since it can vary in magnitude from one processing machine to another or from the same machine run at different speeds. A color check might be made initially on a vinyl calender running slowly, the color could be O.K.'d, then change completely when the remainder of the run is made at production speeds. Cases of mottling in a brushed paint finish arising from this effect have been reported. A similar, but much more subtle effect has been noticed with molybdate oranges. Some organic pigment crystals are known to exhibit a dichroic effect, a change in color with different crystal orientation (5). This could conceivably lead to problems in practice, although none have been reported to date.

Colorant concentrations, when varied over wide ranges, can introduce geometric effects and difficulties in visual vs. colorimetric evaluation. Materials with low colorant concentrations can approach a volume mode of perception—i.e., the color is seen within a transparent volume rather than on a surface. High concentrations can contribute surface effects similar to the type encountered with non-glossy surfaces. Also, if colorant particles protrude from the medium, as is the case with many latex paints, a change of the refractive index relationship results.

One effect, not geometrical, but certainly a visual complication, is that of colorant metamerism. It cannot be given justice here since it has been a subject of many papers and even a conference, but it must be at least mentioned. Essentially a pair of colors matched with differing colorants and therefore differing spectral curves can give, under certain illumination conditions, a color match, either visual or instrumental. Under other conditions, the match may fail miserably. In other words, it is an illuminant conditional match.

Metallic Finishes

One of the most interesting areas where geometric effects play an important part is that of metallic finishes. It is one of the few places in which a color match breakdown with change of illumination or viewing geometry is the goal. This property is sometimes loosely referred to as "geometric metamerism." A body of knowledge, largely empirical, has been built up around the control of this effect. This control is still far from a science, however.

Essentially, metallic flakes are added to a medium pigmented with transparent or nearly transparent colorants. The flakes, normally aluminum, tend to orient themselves parallel with the surface. The effect desired is a brilliantly colored topflash at normal illumination and viewing and a hue or chroma shift with the loss of metallic flash on oblique viewing or down flop. The size distribution of metal particles can be used to control the chroma difference between topflash and downflop. Larger particles lighten the top and give a dark, colorless downflop, whereas finer distributions carry color around to the side and give a less harsh effect. Extreme fines in metallic powders also contribute a whitish gray to the downflop since they do not act as a metallic pigment at this orientation and size. The relative transparency of the colorants in these mixtures can also control the location of color between topflash and downflop. In general, the opaque, scattering colorants reach a maximum effect on the downflop, and the transparents reach their maximum on the topflash. For example, small additions of white pigment to a metallic lighten the top appearance very slightly, but the downflop is whitened to a great degree. This effect of varying pigment transparency brings up the concept, as discouraging as it may seem to pigment and dispersion people, of using varying degrees of dispersion as a control factor in formulating metallics. To hold color in the top of a metallic, the best dispersion should be used. To drop the color, or just one component of the color, around to the downflop, a less critical dispersion can be used.

The effect of surface texture on metallics is essentially the same as that encountered with non-metallics, but many phenomena are accentuated. Extremely rough textures blend the topflash and downflop and may in some cases almost cancel the effect. This arises not only from the disturbance of the parallel orientation of the metallic flakes but also from the diffusing effect of the rough surface on emerging radiation.

Some colorimetric data and spectrophotometric curves have been accumulated recently in an attempt to demonstrate this effect (2). However, the whole subject of metallics deserves considerable study to get away from empiricism.

The practicing color technologist must be aware of many interfering but important visual effects in his attempts to apply colorimetry to his daily work. Much remains to be done in formulation of theories and methods for exact definition and control of these visual effects.

Literature Cited

(1) Foster, R. S., *Color Eng.* **1965,** 3 (4), 21.
(2) Johnston, R., *Color Eng.* **1967,** 5 (3), 42.
(3) Judd, D. B., *Color Eng.* **1964,** 2 (5), 14.
(4) OSA Committee on Colorimetry, "Science of Color," Chap. 5, Crowell, 1953.
(5) Patterson, D., "Pigments, An Introduction to Their Physical Chemistry," p. 59, Elsevier, New York, 1967.
(6) Saunderson, J. L., *J. Opt. Soc. Am.* **1942,** 32 (12), 727.

RECEIVED May 18, 1970.

Instrumentation for Color Measurement

FRED W. BILLMEYER, JR.

Rensselaer Polytechnic Institute, Troy, N. Y. 12181

Modern photoelectric color-measuring instruments include: (a) spectrophotometers, with which the spectral reflectance curve of the sample is determined and CIE tristimulus values—the usual end result of color measurement—are obtained by simultaneous or subsequent integration; (b) colorimeters, in which the combination of the spectral-power distribution of the instrument source and the spectral response of its photodetector are adjusted by modifying filters to make the instrument approximately direct reading in CIE coordinates within linear transformations. The appropriate use of colorimeters is the measurement of small color differences between similar samples. This paper describes typical color-measuring spectrophotometers and tristimulus colorimeters and discusses their precision and accuracy for measuring color coordinates and color differences.

Foster and Johnston (*20, 28*) have described the physical, psychophysical, and psychological aspects of the phenomenon we call color and have provided the mathematical framework on which to base the simulation of color vision to rate color judgments numerically as one attribute of appearance. This paper considers the principles of operation and the construction of instruments for obtaining these numerical data.

First, however, why is instrumental color specification important, and how can we hope to provide numbers correlating with so personal an experience as color vision? One answer lies in the need in many operations and transactions involving color, in business, science, and industry, to be able to express in numbers at least some part of what we see. The human eye is not well adapted to providing quantitative information about color—e.g., about the small difference in color between two similar objects. In fact, it has surprising limitations for even the qualitative prediction of the nature of small color differences (*35*).

One reasonable objective for the instrumental specification of color is, therefore, to provide both qualitative and quantitative information on the nature and size of small color differences. To this may be added the desirability of providing a quantitative memory for color, which the eye and brain possess only to a limited degree (3).

Although quantification is often taken to be the essence of measurement, another point of view can be argued. In a recent paper on standards of measurement (2), A. V. Astin describes color measurement as a scheme of classification related primarily to the properties of the human eye. I interpret this to refer to the fact that no instrument can measure color, which is truly a psychological phenomenon, but only certain physical quantities which, one hopes, correlate with what we call color. The primary purpose of this article is to explore the measurement of these physical variables. We must, however, touch upon the question of the validity of such measurements, defined (9) as the extent of agreement between the results of the physical measurements and the corresponding visual observations.

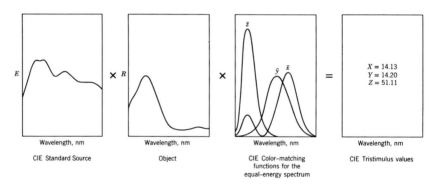

F. W. Billmeyer, M. Saltzman, "Principles
of Color Technology," Interscience

Figure 1.   The CIE tristimulus values X, Y, and Z are obtained by multiplying together the relative power E of a CIE standard illuminant, the reflectance R of an object, and the color-matching functions x̄, ȳ, z̄ of the CIE standard observer, followed by summing up over the visible spectrum

The physical quantities important in specifying color are the spectral-power distribution of the light source (often a CIE standard source), the spectral reflectance of the sample, and the spectral response of the eye in the form of color-matching functions, conveniently those defining the CIE standard observer, designated x̄, ȳ, and z̄. As indicated in Figure 1, the multiplication of these quantities together, wavelength by wavelength, followed by summation across the visible spectrum, gives the CIE tristimulus values X, Y, and Z. In almost all instances, these values or the chromaticity coordinates x and y plus the luminance Y [where $x = X/(X + Y + Z)$ and $y = Y/(X + Y + Z)$] form the desired result of color measurement.

In considering the validity of instrumental color measurement, it is necessary to inquire how well both the instrument and the conditions of visual observation correspond to the CIE standard conditions, including the characteristics of the light source and the observer, and in addition the illuminating and viewing geometry. These points are considered.

Neither the visual nor the instrumental result can be any better than the sample which is measured. Often, too little attention is paid to selection of the sample and to the question of how well it represents the material to be tested (11).

Finally, the concept of describing such a complex phenomenon as color, which is only a small part of the total appearance of a sample, by the specification of only three variables such as the CIE tristimulus values, is a gross oversimplification. Our only hope that there will be agreement between the observations and the measurements lies in simplifying and restricting the visual situation so as to hold constant the many variables not accounted for by the measurements in the present state of their development. These variables include but are not limited to the nature of the surround, the size and spatial separation of the samples, and the field of view they subtend at the eye. These restrictions are, however, no more severe than those applied in careful visual work, as for example in the observations of small color differences recently encouraged by the CIE (12, 36).

Instrumentation Concepts Applied to Color Measurements

Before illustrating some of the equipment currently used for color measurement, I review instrumentation practice in this field from a generic approach, drawing extensively on recent work by Bentley (4). Although reflectance measurement is referred to throughout, much of what is said applies to transmittance measurement as well.

Illuminating and Viewing Geometry. One of the most important initial considerations in designing a color-measuring instrument deals with the presentation of the sample to the light source and detector. That is, what is the geometry by which the incident illumination is introduced onto the sample and by which the reflected light is collected and transmitted to the detector? There are, of course, many ways in which this can be done, but in practice a limited number of sets of illuminating and viewing conditions have been accepted by industry as standard. These fall into three categories.

The first is illumination and viewing by nearly collimated light at fixed angles. By convention, the illumination angle is normal to the sample (designated 0°) and the viewing angle is at 45° to the normal (Figure 2); this is termed normal/45° geometry. The reverse—illumination at 45° and viewing along the normal (45°/normal geometry)—is often considered optically equivalent by virtue of Helmholtz's reversibility principle. This may or may not be the case, depending on the surface texture of the sample and other variables (18).

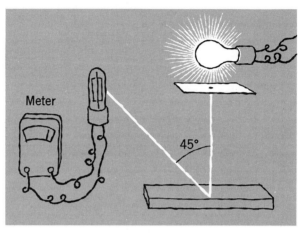

Figure 2.   Arrangement of instrument components illustrating normal/45° geometry

The second set of illuminating and viewing conditions in common use involves the concept of diffuse illumination or viewing. In diffuse illumination, light is incident on the sample in equal amounts from each of all possible angles, whereas in diffuse viewing, all of the light reflected from the sample is collected and delivered to the detector. I know of no way in which both of these can be done simultaneously; in practice, diffuse viewing is often combined with normal or near-normal illumination [the reverse conditions are usually equivalent (15)] in the device known as the integrating sphere (Figure 3). This is a hollow cavity, usually spherical or nearly so, lined with a diffusely reflecting white material. As Figure 3 shows, the detector is placed so as to view the interior of the sphere, illuminated by all the light reflected from the sample, but the detector does not see the sample or the light source directly.

A third illuminating-viewing geometry, which to date has been included in only a few instruments (17, 23), is that which may be described as goniophotometric illumination and viewing, in which the sample is illuminated and viewed with collimated light as in the 45°/normal and normal/45° geometries, but in which the angles are variable. Data from

F. W. Billmeyer, M. Saltzman, "Principles
of Color Technology," Interscience

Figure 3.   Reflectance measurement with an integrating sphere used in near-normal/diffuse geometry. Here the specular (mirror) reflection is removed by a gloss trap; alternately, it can be included if the trap is replaced by part of the sphere wall.

goniophotometric instruments may be collected over a range of these angles, and it is expected that the use of such instruments will provide an understanding of such problems as goniochromatism or geometric metamerism (23, 27).

Since the CIE has provided so much of the basic standardization for color measurement, we should indicate its stand on illuminating and viewing geometry. In 1931 the CIE recommended the use of 45°/normal conditions, but the suitability of the integrating-sphere geometry to the requirements of instrumentation has led over the intervening years to its widespread adoption. Over the same period, the question of which type correlates better with the usual visual situation has not been resolved, and at present some groups favor each geometry. In 1967, in an effort to encourage standardization within each major type, the CIE adopted (12, 36) a recommendation specifying four geometries: 45°/normal, normal/45°, diffuse/normal, and normal/diffuse. Most current color-measuring instruments conform to one of the four categories of the new CIE recommendation.

Nature of Illuminating Light. The expression of the results of color measurement in terms compatible with the visual perception of color requires modification of the spectral character of the light reaching the detector. That is, somewhere in the instrument there must be provision for selecting certain broad or narrow bands of wavelengths out of the whole visible spectrum and detecting these wavelengths alone. If there were no contraindications, this selection could de done at any stage of the process. Taking the 45°/normal geometry as an example (Figure 4), it would be possible to modify the light (by filters in this case) either before or after it reaches the sample. For most materials, either option would be satisfactory, but if the sample is fluorescent, only the latter can be used for the following reason.

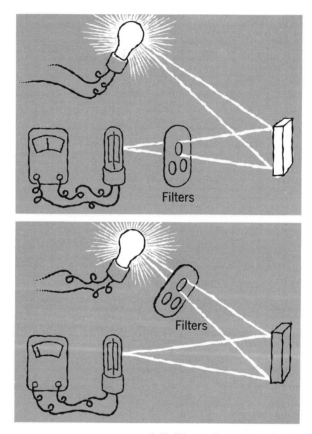

F. W. Billmeyer, M. Saltzman, "Principles
of Color Technology," Interscience

Figure 4. Two possible locations for light-modifying filters illustrated for 45°/normal geometry

A fluorescent sample is one which absorbs light of short wavelengths (often in the ultraviolet or the blue end of the visible spectrum) and emits it at longer wavelengths in the visible region. The perceived color of such a sample will result from the effect on the eye of all the light reaching it: some reflected, some emitted as the result of fluorescence, both portions recognized as having their proper colors as well as proper relative amounts.

In an instrument built with the filters or other modifiers between the source and the sample, the following can happen. Suppose the sample is being illuminated by blue light. Because the filter selector or wavelength dial is set for blue, one assumes that the detector response corresponds to blue light only. However, if the sample absorbs some of the blue light and fluoresces in the red portion of the spectrum, what the detector sees is a combination of blue plus red, and it does not differentiate the components of this combination properly. Thus, a false indication is received.

Today, many materials are deliberately made fluorescent. "Optical whiteners" are added in vast amounts to white fabrics, soaps and detergents, papers, and many other products. It is becoming more and more important in the manufacture of color-measuring equipment to illuminate the sample appropriately for fluorescent materials.

Sources and Source Simulation. Various light sources are encouncountered every day. We are all familiar with incandescent electric lamps, fluorescent-tube lighting, and the many variations of natural daylight. Fortunately, international agreement has been reached which limits the number of such sources which must be considered for color measurement. Those recommended by the CIE include an incandescent lamp operating at about 2850 K and a series of sources representing natural daylight. To date, the CIE has made no recommendations regarding fluorescent lamps.

To go further one must recall the CIE-recommended definitions of 2 terms: a source of light is defined as a real, physical lamp, whereas the word illuminant refers to a spectral-power distribution, which may or may not be physically realizable. For example, the particular overcast-sky daylight outside my office window is a source, but not an illuminant because its spectral-power distribution is not known. On the other hand, average daylight can be defined accurately by its spectral-power distribution as an illuminant, but it is not readily available as a natural source.

The 1931 recommendations of the CIE included sources B and C representing noon sunlight and overcast-sky daylight, respectively. These sources, realizable by incandescent lamp-filter combinations, are deficient compared with natural daylight in their ultraviolet light content. With the increasing importance of fluorescent materials, the CIE recommended in 1964 supplementing sources B and C (subsequently defined also as illuminants) with a new series of illuminants based on average daylight, the most important of which has a correlated color temperature of 6500 K (illuminant D_{65}), with others at 5500 and 7500 K. These illuminants are defined in the ultraviolet wavelength range as well as the visible (specifically, from 300 to 860 nm) and thus are recommended for use whenever fluorescent materials are to be measured. Ultimately, it is expected that the use of B and C will no longer be recommended.

The net result of these deliberations is that an important objective for instrument manufacturers is the development of sources whose spectral-power output closely matches that defining the CIE's new daylight illuminants, including the ultraviolet range. This can be done in at least two ways: by using a properly filtered xenon-arc lamp or by the appropriate combination of stable filters with a tungsten-halogen lamp operating at a color temperature of 3100 K. Figure 5 compares the spectral-power distribution of an illuminator of the second type with that of CIE illuminant D_{65}, as a state-of-the-art example of how well this simulation of daylight can currently be accomplished. The use of such illuminators should greatly facilitate the development of accurate and valid procedures for the color measurement of fluorescent materials.

Comparison Methods: Sample *vs*. Standard. Let us now turn to the problem of how to compare light reflected from a sample with that from a standard. Depending on circumstances, the standard may be a white reference material, or it may be very similar to the sample.

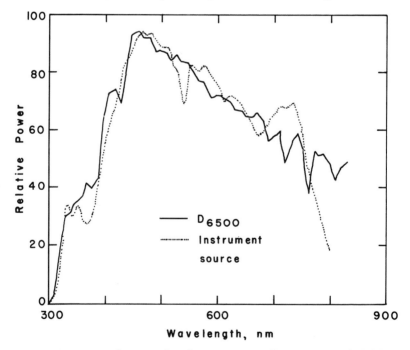

Figure 5. Spectral power distribution of CIE Illuminant D_{65} (solid line) and its simulation over the wavelength range 300–800 nm by a 3100 K incandescent lamp plus filters (4)

Visually, one almost always judges sample and standard side by side, looking rapidly from one to the other. The same conditions can be realized in an instrument. Quite often, this is done by utilizing integrating-sphere geometry in which the sample and standard are placed at two symmetrically located ports in a single sphere (Figure 6). The illumination (or viewing, depending on which variant of the integrating-sphere geometry is used) is rapidly alternated between sample and standard, for example 30 to 60 times per second. Thus, the detector responds alternately to the sample and standard, and the two are compared in effect by restandardizing the instrument every 1/30 to 1/60 second.

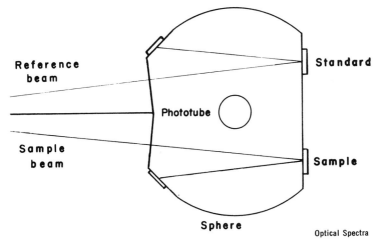

Optical Spectra

Figure 6. Arrangement of an integrating sphere used in double-beam operation (13)

Instruments built according to this double-beam principle can be quite stable and accurate but are inherently expensive. As an alternate, there is a simpler method, in which the sample and standard are viewed sequentially. This would never be done in visual practice for the unreliability of the memory for color is well known (3). However, the stability of instrument components is such that with single illuminating and viewing beams, as in Figures 2–4, measurement can be made by what is known as the substitution method. The standard is first placed in the measuring position, and the instrument is adjusted to give readings corresponding to its calibrated values. Then the standard is removed, and the sample is placed in the measuring position. The instrument readings are now representative of the sample, provided that the calibration of the instrument has not changed since the standardization.

Photometry. Comparison must be made between the electrical signals generated when the sample and standard are presented to the photo-

detector in a color-measuring instrument. Two basically different methods
for this photometric comparison are shown in Figure 7, which is based
on double-beam geometry as a convenient illustration.

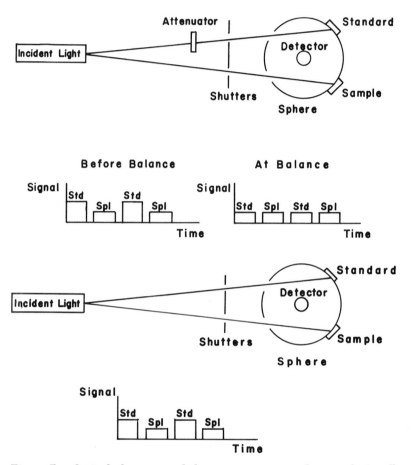

*Figure 7. Optical elements and detector output signals typical of null
(top) and direct photometry (bottom) (4)*

In the null method (Figure 7 top), light falls alternately on the sample and standard. The detector output signal, idealized, is a series of
alternating pulses with heights proportional to the reflectances of the
sample and standard. The difference in these heights is reduced to zero,
either manually or automatically, by a calibrated light attenuator located
in the standard beam. The attenuator may be a mechanical device such
as a slit or "comb," or an optical element such as a pair of polarizers. At
the balance or null point, the ratio of the reflectance of the sample to

that of the standard is given by the setting of the attenuator. The accuracy of the measurement depends on the calibration of the attenuator.

The second method of photometry is similar, except that the attenuator does not exist. Here the reflectance of the sample relative to that of the standard is given directly by the ratio of the corresponding detector signals, measured electrically. The accuracy of the measurement depends on the linearity of the photodetector and the calibration of the associated electronic circuitry.

Data Reduction. This section deals with the problem of converting the instrument signals, proportional to the amount of some kind of light reflected from the sample, into color coordinates bearing some relation to visual perception. This is data reduction in its broad sense, though the term is often used to refer solely to computational aspects of the process.

Almost universally, instrument designers have elected to present data in the form of, or in a form readily derived from or convertible to, CIE tristimulus values X, Y, and Z. The equations for defining these coordinates are:

$$X = \Sigma \, E \, R \, \bar{x}$$
$$Y = \Sigma \, E \, R \, \bar{y}$$
$$Z = \Sigma \, E \, R \, \bar{z}$$

where E is the spectral power of a CIE standard source, R the spectral reflectance of the sample, and $\bar{x}$, $\bar{y}$, and $\bar{z}$ are the spectral color-matching functions defining the CIE standard observer. All these quantities vary with the wavelength of the light, and the summations are carried out at definite intervals of wavelength, such as 10 nm, across the visible spectrum. (Normalization factors have for the moment been omitted, and the basic definitions of X, Y, and Z as integrals have been bypassed in favor of the approximating summations.)

Since E and $\bar{x}$, $\bar{y}$, and $\bar{z}$ are tabulated in numerical form, one way of solving these equations is to measure R as a function of wavelength and carry out the summations numerically as indicated. This is practiced widely. One uses a reflectance spectrophotometer as the measuring instrument. The summations can be performed in many different ways: on a desk calculator or a digital computer or by accessory tristimulus integrators attached to the instrument. Both analog and digital computer accessories are commercially available.

Since spectrophotometers are basically expensive instruments, one looks for an alternate and simpler approach. One way to do this is to introduce the quantities E, $\bar{x}$, $\bar{y}$, and $\bar{z}$ optically rather than numerically, by broad-band filters, adjusting the combination of the instrument's detector response and source power distribution to be equivalent to the combination of the CIE color-matching detector responses and the power

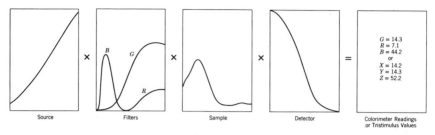

F. W. Billmeyer, M. Saltzman, ''Principles
of Color Technology,'' Interscience

Figure 8. In colorimetry, instrument readings convertible to CIE tristimulus values by simple linear transformation (to a first approximation) are obtained from measurements with the instrument's response (light source times filter times detector) adjusted to the combination (CIE standard source times CIE standard observer) sketched in Figure 1

distribution of a CIE standard source. Figures 1 and 8 illustrate the process.

This approach leads to instruments known as tristimulus colorimeters. In effect, they are optical analog computers for producing the CIE tristimulus values. In general, they are less expensive but less accurate than spectrophotometer-computer combinations, and because of their inherent low accuracy they are usually limited in application to the comparison of a sample and a standard which are nearly alike—in other words, to color-difference measurement.

Accuracy. The requirements for accuracy in color measurement are different from those for other applications of the instruments involved. Analytical spectrophotometry, for example, emphasizes the accurate determination of the wavelengths of absorption bands; photometric accuracy is often secondary. In reflectance spectrophotometry for color measurement the opposite is required: most colored materials have gently-sloping absorption bands, so that high wavelength accuracy is of less importance, but the requirements on photometric accuracy are formidable.

For example, let us consider the magnitude of change in reflectance level required to produce a just-perceptible difference in color. This varies widely with the reflectance level of the sample. For a high reflectance white, one can just see a difference of 0.4% in reflectance, easily measured by most instruments. However, at the dark-gray level of 10% reflectance, a change of 0.05% (absolute) can be seen, and at the low but useful level of 1% reflectance (attained in navy blues and many other dark colors over much of their reflectance curve) one can detect a change in reflectance of around 0.01%. I know of no instrument that can measure reflectance at the 1% level with a precision of ±0.01%. Thus, there are still some challenges to be met in the design of instruments for color measurement.

Characteristics of Modern Color-Measuring Instruments

This section describes a limited number of popular color-measuring instruments selected to illustrate the principles just discussed. Only brief reference is made to other examples, and no attempt is made to be complete. Finally, some remarks are made on the problems of obtaining satisfactory precision and accuracy in color measurement.

Spectrophotometers. For many years the referee instrument for accurate color measurement has been the General Electric (Hardy) recording spectrophotometer (*22*). The following description is based on the newer (*32*) commercial model (Figure 9). The instrument utilizes a double prism monochromator to produce light containing only a narrow band of wavelengths, approximately 10 nm wide. The light from the monochromator is split into two beams, arranged (Figure 10) so that the standard and sample are illuminated alternately. An integrating sphere is used in near-normal/diffuse geometry. The photometer is the null-balance type, the attenuator operating on the polarization principle. The photometric linearity of one instrument was demonstrated (*33*) to be better than ±0.1%. Since 1968 the instrument has been supplied with a photomultiplier detector and solid-state amplifier replacing the phototube and Plexiglas rod indicated in Figure 10, with a significant improvement in sensitivity.

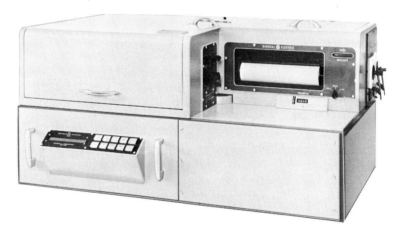

F. W. Billmeyer, M. Saltzman, "Principles of Color Technology," Interscience

Figure 9.   The new model General Electric spectrophotometer

Because of its illuminating-viewing geometry, the General Electric spectrophotometer is not suited for measuring fluorescent samples, and the simulation of standard sources is not relevant. The precision and accuracy of this instrument have been studied (*8*) and are discussed later.

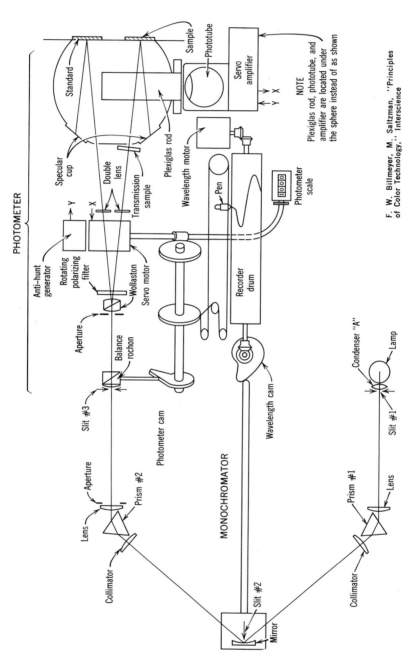

Figure 10. Essential components of the General Electric spectrophotometer

F. W. Billmeyer, M. Saltzman, "Principles of Color Technology," Interscience

A recently announced instrument, the Trilac spectrophotometer (*23*) (Kollmorgen), is of particular interest for color measurement because of the flexibility of its illuminating and viewing geometry. In addition to both normal/diffuse and diffuse/normal integrating-sphere geometries, it offers goniophotometric illumination and viewing for the first time in a commercial instrument.

Other spectrophotometers commonly used for color measurement (Bausch and Lomb, Beckman, Cary) are analytical instruments to which a reflectance accessory has been added. Such an arrangement has, in instruments so far produced, not been as successful as designing specifically for color measurement (for example, Kollmorgen Trilac, Zeiss).

Since most colored samples have relatively gently sloping spectral reflectance curves, a continuous recording of this curve is not always

F. W. Billmeyer, M. Saltzman,
"Principles of Color Technology"
Interscience

Figure 11.   Hunter D25 color and color difference meter

essential. Values of the reflectance at a limited number of specified wavelengths are often sufficient for calculating the tristimulus values. In the technique of abridged spectrophotometry, a series of narrow band interference filters, often passing a band of wavelengths 5–10 nm wide, is used to obtain these reflectances. In some instances colorimeters are equipped with such filters, as mentioned later.

For automatic data reduction to tristimulus values, the spectrophotometer can be utilized with a digital readout unit (6) (Datex), providing data punched on cards or tape for direct access to a digital computer or with accessory tristimulus integrators of the analog or digital type (Kollmorgen, Librascope).

Colorimeters. Typical of colorimeters utilizing 45°/normal geometry is the Hunter Associates Laboratory D-25 color and color-difference meter (24). [Other instruments of this general type are manufactured by Gardner, Martin-Sweets, Meeco, Neotec.] The Hunter instrument is a single-

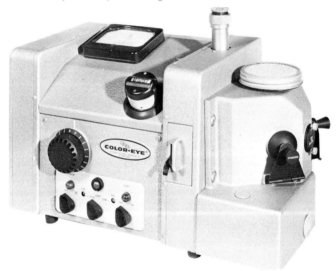

F. W. Billmeyer, M. Saltzman, "Principles
of Color Technology," Interscience

Figure 12.   Kollmorgen D-1 Color-Eye

beam colorimeter (Figure 11) in which standard and sample are measured sequentially. The instrument is direct reading in color scales more nearly representing equal steps of visual perception than do the CIE coordinates: a lightness value $L = 10\sqrt{Y}$ and chromaticity coordinates $a(+a =$ redness; $-a =$ greenness) and $b(+b =$ yellowness, $-b =$ blueness).

Most colorimeters of this type illuminate the sample with white light so that fluorescent specimens can be measured, but accurate simulation of CIE standard sources is not common. The Hunter instrument uses direct photometry; other modifications are also utilized.

The Kollmorgen D-1 Color-Eye is a double-beam integrating-sphere colorimeter (Figure 12) utilizing a nonstandard diffuse/near-45° geometry. The model LS Color-Eye is similar but uses an 18-inch diameter integrating sphere with diffuse/normal geometry. Accurate simulation of a standard source is not normal, but special daylight illuminators (Figure 5) are under development. A mechanical slit attenuator is used. The instrument is equipped with 16 interference filters for abridged spectrophotometry. [Another integrating-sphere colorimeter is manufactured by Zeiss.]

A feature of major interest in colorimeters is the degree to which their source–filter–photodetector response curves duplicate those of a CIE standard illuminant (usually C) and the CIE standard observer.

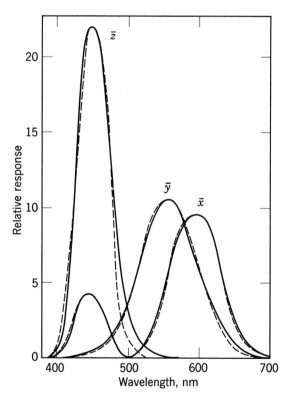

F. W. Billmeyer, M. Saltzman, "Principles of Color Technology," Interscience

Figure 13.   CIE standard observer functions $\bar{x}$, $\bar{y}$, $\bar{z}$ (solid lines) and their simulation by the source-filter-phototube combination of a colorimeter specially calibrated for close conformance to the CIE system

Both the instruments described above, and others, are individually calibrated in this respect; the results achievable (30) can be illustrated by attributing all the residual error to the standard observer functions and comparing them with the CIE $\bar{x}$, $\bar{y}$, and $\bar{z}$ curves (Figure 13). The accuracy achievable in this way is discussed later.

Standards and Calibration. A color-measuring instrument in good operating condition requires, as a minimum, only a reference white standard to ensure correct results. Since 1931 the white standard recommended by the CIE has been smoked MgO, but on Jan. 1, 1969, this reference was changed to the perfect diffuser (12, 36). For practical reasons, smoked MgO is often replaced by another white reference material, more easily prepared and more stable, such as pressed $BaSO_4$, used as a working standard. To obtain CIE tristimulus values referred to the perfect diffuser, it is necessary to apply a correction to measured values, based on knowledge of the reflectance of the working standard with the perfect diffuser as 100. For highest accuracy, the correction must be applied to spectral reflectances; colorimeter readings obviously cannot be so adjusted. A major step toward solving the white-standard problem has recently been achieved with the production (21) of $BaSO_4$ with reflectance near 99.9% of that of the perfect diffuser over a major part of the visible spectrum (14), good reproducibility from lot to lot, and excellent aging characteristics (Eastman white reflectance standard).

In addition to the white reference standard, other calibrated samples are required to ensure that color-measuring instruments are in good working order. This problem is not solved completely, although research is active and some standards are commercially available (25, 29) (Hunterlabs, Kollmorgen, NBS).

Precision and Accuracy. The precision and accuracy of industrial color measurement have been discussed (8, 9, 10, 26). The results are described best in terms of color-difference units (31) on a scale such that one unit is approximately the smallest color difference perceptible under normal conditions. The published results can be summarized as follows.

The repeatability of color measurement with a single instrument is usually quite good, corresponding in many cases to 95% confidence limits of less than one unit of color difference, even over long periods of time. The reproducibility among a group of instruments of the same make and model is often much less satisfactory. For the General Electric spectrophotometer, as an example, it ranged from two to six color-difference units for light colors to 10–15 units for dark, high chroma samples.

Taking the General Electric instrument as the referee instrument, a group of colorimeters with individual calibrations for conformance to the CIE system had an average accuracy of 2.5–16 units, depending on sample type and illuminating-viewing geometry (16). Their performance in color-difference measurement was, of course, much better, and this is the type of measurement most appropriate to colorimeters in contrast to spectrophotometers (7). Even here, caution is required since color-difference measurement based on tristimulus values alone, as with a colorimeter, is appropriate only if there is no metamerism between sample and standard (5). This important point is often overlooked.

Summary

Sometimes for expedience, sometimes for convenience, and often because of the varied requirements of different color-measurement problems, many different types of color-measuring instruments are in use. The major distinction between types is that of spectrophotometers *vs.* tristimulus colorimeters.

In one respect the function of these two instrument types is similar for after data reduction both furnish the tristimulus values of the sample. Actually, however, the spectrophotometer provides much more information in the form of the spectral reflectance curve of the sample. There are many important areas of color technology which depend on this information. Among them are the detection and control of metamerism (20) and the formulation of mixtures of colorants (dyes, pigments) having specified colors (1).

In other areas, the tristimulus values alone suffice, and either type of instrument can be used. Because of their simplicity and lower cost, tristimulus colorimeters are used more often for color-difference measurement, but spectrophotometers will do this job just as well if available. Moreover, some colorimeters are now equipped with a series of interference filters so that they are additionally abridged spectrophotometers, providing both diagnostic and quantitative information on the spectral reflectance curve.

Finally, major unsolved problems in color measurement still exist, not the least of which is the provision of instruments whose performance can equal in precision and accuracy, for all sorts of colors, the standard set by the human eye. Since color is only one of many aspects of appearance (20) and since the measurements we can make approximate only roughly the variables of perceived color (19), I firmly believe that we shall never pass beyond the situation in which "the eye is the final arbiter; the instrument the aid (34).

Acknowledgment

I am greatly indebted to George P. Bentley, Kollmorgen Corp., for helpful discussions on the generic approach to the principles of color-measuring instrumentation. This is Contribution No. 25 from the Rensselaer Color Measurement Laboratory, whose work is supported in part by the Dry Color Manufacturer's Association and the Paint Research Institute.

Literature Cited

(1) Allen, E., ADVAN. CHEM. SER. 1971, 107, 87.
(2) Astin, A. V., *Sci. Am.* 1968, 218 (6), 50.
(3) Bartleson, C. J., *J. Opt. Soc. Am.* 1960, 50, 73.
(4) Bentley, G. P., *New England Sect., Opt. Soc. Am.* (May 23, 1968).
(5) Berger, A., Brockes, A., *Color Eng.* 1967, 5 (3), 34.
(6) Billmeyer, F. W., Jr., *J. Opt. Soc. Am.* 1960, 50, 137.
(7) Billmeyer, F. W., Jr., *Official Digest* 1962, 34, 1333.
(8) Billmeyer, F. W., Jr., *J. Opt. Soc. Am.* 1965, 55, 707.
(9) Billmeyer, F. W., Jr., *J. Paint Technol.* 1966, 38, 726.
(10) Billmeyer, F. W., Jr., *Color Eng.* 1966, 4 (4), 15.
(11) Billmeyer, F. W., Jr., *J. Paint Technol.* 1967, 39, 342.
(12) Billmeyer, F. W., Jr., *Color Eng.* 1968, 6 (1), 34.
(13) Billmeyer, F. W., Jr., *Optical Spectra* 1968, 2 (4), 76.
(14) Billmeyer, F. W., Jr., *Appl. Opt.* 1969, 8, 737.
(15) Billmeyer, F. W., Jr., Marcus, R. T., *Appl. Opt.* 1969, 8, 763.
(16) Billmeyer, F. W., Jr., *Appl. Opt.* 1969, 8, 775.
(17) Billmeyer, F. W., Jr., Davidson, J. G., *J. Paint Technol.* 1969, 41, 647.
(18) Billmeyer, F. W., Jr., *Proc. Intern. Colour Assoc.*, "Color 69," Stockholm, in press.
(19) Evans, R. M., *J. Opt. Soc. Am.* 1964, 54, 1467.
(20) Foster, R. S., ADVAN. CHEM. SER. 1971, 107, 17.
(21) Grum, F., Luckey, G. W., *Appl. Opt.* 1968, 7, 2289.
(22) Hardy, A. C., *J. Opt. Soc. Am.* 1935, 25, 305.
(23) Hemmendinger, H., Johnston, R. M., *Proc. Intern. Colour Assoc.*, "Color 69," Stockholm, in press.
(24) Hunter, R. S., *J. Opt. Soc. Am.* 1958, 48, 985.
(25) Hunter, R. S., *J. Opt. Soc. Am.* 1963, 53, 390.
(26) Illing, A. M., Balinkin, I., *Am. Ceramic Soc. Bull.* 1965, 44, 12.
(27) Johnston, R. M., *Color Eng.* 1967, 5 (3), 42.
(28) Johnston, R. M., ADVAN. CHEM. SER. 1971, 107, 4.
(29) Keegan, H. J., Schleter, J. C., Judd, D. B., *J. Res. Natl. Bur. Stds.* 1962, 66A, 203.
(30) Lewis, E. L., *Color Eng.* 1967, 5 (5), 37.
(31) MacAdam, D. L., ADVAN. CHEM. SER. 1971, 107, 69.
(32) Pritchard, B. S., Holmwood, W. A., *J. Opt. Soc. Am.* 1955, 45, 690.
(33) Rhodes, E. C., Billmeyer, F. W., Jr., *Appl. Opt.* 1969, 8, 769.
(34) Saltzman, M., *Color Eng.* 1963, 1 (4), 12.
(35) Thurner, K., "Colorimetry in Textile Dyeing—Theory and Practice," Badische Aniline- & Soda-Fabrik, 1965.
(36) Wyszecki, G., *J. Opt. Soc. Am.* 1968, 58, 290.

RECEIVED June 6, 1969.

The Perception of Color

RALPH M. EVANS

Eastman Kodak Co., Rochester, N. Y. 14650

The science of colorimetry—i.e., the science of measuring color—is based on two facts: (1) all possible hues can be produced by using only three colored lights, and (2) two colors which match do not necessarily have the same spectral energy distribution. Color is only one small aspect of appearance. Other aspects include such characteristics as glossiness, opacity, smoothness, metallic reflection, and roughness. These appearance characteristics, however, will not affect the color of an object. Five basic differences can be seen between colors. For light sources and isolated colors there are three—hue, saturation, and brightness. For object colors there are four—hue, saturation, gray content, and lightness. For illumination, there are all five. It takes four dimensions to represent all object color perceptions, and it takes a series of three-dimensional spaces to illustrate them.

What do we see when we look at a color? How can colors vary? What does this variation mean in terms of how we can describe colors? To answer these questions, we must go back 300 years to when Newton discovered that all possible hues could be produced by using only three colored lights. One hundred years ago Helmholtz and Maxwell discovered that two colors which match do not necessarily have the same spectral energy distribution. These two facts form the basis of the science of colorimetry—the science of measuring color. This science has developed largely within this century, and this development has been international. Colorimetry gives us the tools to calculate numbers which will predict whether or not two colors will match in a given illumination and whether or not they will continue to match in different illuminations with respect to international standards. It is an important science for those who must use color commercially and will be used more widely in the future. The science of colorimetry, however, is not intended to and does not predict what a given color will look like except under the simplest of situations. The appearance of color is the subject of this paper. Although some firmly held beliefs will be questioned, the fundamentals of this science are in no way questioned.

Fundamental to and parallel with the development of colorimetry is the implicit assumption: since all colors can be produced by using three lights, all possible perceived colors can be arranged in a three-dimensional space. Although the truth of this statement remains unquestioned, it is quite obviously wrong. All possible perceived colors cannot be represented in a three-dimensional space. It is just this assumption that has made the subject of color perception so confusing both to scientists and artists.

Perceived Color

Color is one small part of the much larger subject of appearance—*i.e.,* the way things look. Figure 1a shows the variables of appearance in such things as glossiness as seen in the blue pitcher and in the rooster, opacity as seen in all three objects, and smoothness as seen in all three. Other possible variables include metallic reflection (Figure 1b) and the roughness shown by the metallic sponge. These are all appearance characteristics and are totally unrelated to color. They may be present in a

Figure 1a

Figure 1b

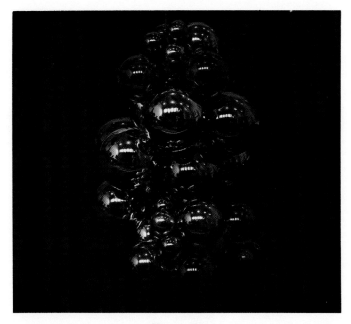

Figure 2a

bewildering variety of combinations, but they will not affect the color of an object.

Most of these appearance characteristics are obvious because the object does not appear to be uniform in color. In Figure 2a both the shape and glossiness of each ball are seen because of the nonuniformity of

Figure 2b

color, yet the color of each is uniform over the entire surface of each object. Figure 2b shows mat objects which are perceived as mat simply because they are not shiny. Even here, however, the color is not uniform, and it is precisely this nonuniformity that permits the shape of the threads to be seen. Even in Figure 3a it is this lack of uniformity of color that permits you to interpret what you see.

Figure 3a

To narrow appearance characteristics to what we mean when we say color, we must first specify that what we are talking about is seen as perfectly uniform over its entire area. Hence, we can eliminate such things as glossiness, roughness, shape, etc. and consider the remaining characteristics. In speaking of color, therefore, we mean only a perfectly uniform area, all of whose parts appear identical; size is irrelevant. Even in restricting this definition to a completely uniform area of an object, there are still two possible appearance characteristics that can be seen. First, the area can be opaque or transparent to various degrees (Figure 3b), but transparency does not affect color. Secondly, the object may diffuse the light as does white paper, or it may be a clear reflecting surface like a mirror. Neither of these is an attribute of color.

Figure 3b

These statements can be illustrated by a single example. Figure 4a shows two glass vases. They are shiny over their entire surfaces. This perception is caused by the reflections of the light source which makes their colors nonuniform at that spot. Figure 4b is the same picture, but these reflections have been painted out, and the vases now appear dull all over. The point is that this effect does not change their color. In other words, in Figure 5a the contents of all four glasses have the same color.

Since appearance characteristics are eliminated, what is left? To oversimplify, what remains is absorption of light in such a way that some

Figure 4a

Figure 4b

colors are removed by the light's falling on the area and some are reflected or transmitted. In looking at such an area, however, the color is not in the object but in our minds. This brings us to a preliminary definition of color—*i.e.*, it is the perception by our minds of the fact that light has been modified by the absorption of some part of its rays.

To carry this further now would be to presuppose much that follows. These concepts have been introduced to point out that white should not be considered a color, and whiteness is not part of the color. A series

Figure 5a

of objects varying from white to clear should be considered to be alike
in that they have no color. In other words, white opaque and clear transparent represent the zero of the color system. They are in the system,
but they represent the starting point, the zero from which all possible
colors diverge.

Grays and blacks, however, as in Figure 5b are considered to
have color; each of these is of a different color, starting from zero at the
right and changing continuously to black at the left. They are referred
to, somewhat ambiguously, as the achromatic colors. Note here again
that there is no distinction made between opaque and transparent—it is
the mental image that is referred to and not the objects.

Figure 5b

Thus far we have discussed what color is not, and since this concept may be new, let us view it from a somewhat different angle. Suppose you view colored slides, one of which shows a landscape with blue sky, rocks, a white church, etc. This is one of the best examples of perceived color. What causes you to see this picture? The camera formed a pattern on the surface of the photographic material. The photographic process registered this pattern and produced mixtures of three dyes which imitate the colors of the objects. This transparency is projected onto the screen by a light source and projector lens. The light is reflected from the screen into your eyes and transmitted as signals to the brain. From this pattern you see objects; from the changed quality of the projector light you see color in the areas representing objects. There are no objects on the screen; there are no colors on the screen. What you see are modifications of light

Figure 6a

from the projector, and these produce color in the mind. The areas that appear as white are seen as such because the quality of the light in that area has not been affected by the slide, and what is actually seen is the white screen. On the slide this area would appear clear, transparent, and colorless, and the other areas would appear colored. A photograph of such a situation is shown in Figure 6a. A color photographic transparency, then, is the nearest objective demonstration of the mental perception of color.

Looked at in another way, color, as I define it, is the effect which a watercolor artist produces in the viewer's eyes by what he adds to his white paper. For white he adds nothing and produces no color; for gray, black, and all other colors he adds something. The paints added to the white paper modify the light which falls on the paper, and this modification is seen as the mental image called color.

Hue

The rest of this paper considers all the ways in which two such mental images of color, produced by light from outside the eye, may be seen to differ from each other. The simplest case is that of an isolated color such as that produced by a traffic light at night in the country or by any light source brighter than its surroundings, such as a neon sign in a dark window.

The most readily detected difference between two such isolated colors, especially if the difference is small, is called hue. It is described by the commonly used color words (red, green, etc.), and most of us agree pretty well on the nomenclature. The total number of hues that can be distinguished is not accurately known, but perhaps under the best conditions it may be as high as 300–500. Of this number, however, only four are unique.

People differ widely in their actual choice of the four unique hues because of color vision differences. They are defined, however, as a red which lies between orange-red and bluish red, a yellow which lies between greenish yellow and reddish yellow, a green that lies between yellowish green and bluish green, and a blue which lies between greenish blue and reddish blue. They are sometimes defined as a red which contains neither blue nor yellow, etc., but to many people the unique red seen alone looks bluish (I prefer the name pink for it), and the unique green looks yellowish. All other possible hues are seen as mixtures of two of these with the restriction that it is not possible to have a hue that appears as a mixture of blue and yellow or of red and green. If blue and yellow or red and green are mixed as lights, they tend to cancel in such a way that one or the other or neither remains visible. It is not possible to produce a mixture in which both can be seen.

With these pairs eliminated as mixtures, the remaining pairs can be arranged in a continuous circle. The intermediate colors lie between the four colors noted previously; the red and yellow give orange, the yellow and green give yellow-green; the green and blue give cyan; and the blue and red give purple. All intermediate hues can be spaced between these, and the spacing can be so arranged that opposite colors are complementary—*i.e.*, they produce white light if mixed properly as lights. Alternately, they can be spaced so that there appear to be equal hue differences between any two. It is not possible to do both precisely. As far as known, such a hue circle represents all possible hues, and any hue can be specified by its position on such a circle. Thus, the first variable—*i.e.*, the first possible difference between two colors—is hue.

Saturation

A second difference between two colors either of the same or different hues is the amount of hue seen. This variable is saturation and is illustrated in Figure 6b which shows increasing amounts of saturation in the same hue (approximately). Saturation is an unfortunate word in this context since it implies a similarity to saturation in chemistry which has a definite maximum at which a given solution is said to be saturated with the solute. There is no similar saturated maximum in color. A better chemical analogy is concentration, and it is helpful to think of color saturation as concentration—hue per square inch, if you like.

Figure 6b

While there is no well-defined upper limit to saturation in color, there is a zero saturation shown in the upper left of Figure 6b. At zero saturation there is no hue perception, and the hue is said to be indeterminate. Since hues can be arranged in a circle and saturation starts at zero and increases, the two can be combined in a circular diagram with zero at the center. To indicate a point on such a diagram, a saturation scale is needed. Such a scale is usually produced by taking equally noticeable intervals of saturation, working with actual samples. A system has been worked out for the Munsell "Book of Color," and on one such chart the spacings of both the hues and the saturations are based on equally noticeable differences, and any circle represents constant saturation which, in this system, is called chroma.

Saturation series in a single hue are not common in nature. However, one example is a blue sky fading to pale blue or even white at the horizon. Such a series is also occasionally found in certain flowers such as those shown in Figure 7a. Remember that saturation is the amount of hue seen and nothing else.

Figure 7a

Brightness

The third observable difference between two isolated colors is brightness. A color can vary from being too dim to be seen to being too bright to look at. Except for difficulties in producing it, as far as perception is concerned such a change can occur for any hue at any saturation. Thus, hue, saturation, and brightness are the three variables of isolated colors, and as far as is known they are the only possibilities. All the colors produced by these variables can be assigned a position in a three-dimensional space, the most convenient one probably being cylindrical as in the Munsell system. This is the classical case and probably forms the basis of the belief that perceived color has only three variables.

However, these three variables cannot be combined to produce a gray or black or a color which is seen to contain gray. To perceive gray or a grayed color, at least one other color must be present. This is the distinction that Ostwald made between related and unrelated colors.

Gray can be seen only as a related color. In fact, for a color to appear to contain gray or actually be gray, it must not only have a background but usually must be darker than that background. Gray, then, is a fourth perceived variable of color which was not present in the isolated colors.

The sensitivity of the eye to light is constantly changing. This adaptation level, as it is called, is changed by what we see, what we have just seen, what is beside what we are seeing, and by how long the length of viewing time. In viewing a particular scene, such as that shown in Figure 7b, one's sensitivity to brightness reaches a steady level set by the brightness of the surrounding light and the average reflectances of the

Figure 7b

nearby objects. Color adaptation is set by the colors in the scene, and these usually average about neutral. This is called a normal viewing situation and is the reference point for all our visual experience. In an unusual situation, however, the eye may be in a very different state, both for brightness and for color. This state is produced by the new conditions and determines what color will be seen from a given stimulus. This can be illustrated by a small screen and a projector. Consider a patch of light on a screen which, as a stimulus, is a fairly good match for noon sunlight. If the room were completely dark, it would appear as achromatic. If it is surrounded directly with the brighter direct light from the projector lamp, however, it will be distinctly blue. This brighter and yellower light has taken over your adaptation, and you tend to see the border as white and the center as blue. If this blue patch is surrounded with colored light, the hue of the blue is shifted to another color. That this effect arises from a change in the eye's sensitivity is easily demonstrated by the phenomenon of after-images.

Figure 8a shows a green cross and a clear field with a dot in the center. If you look steadily at the center of this cross, count slowly to 20, and then look at the dot, you will see the change in the sensitivity of your eyes that this green cross has produced. This is an after-image; note its color. That it is a true shift in color sensitivity of your eyes is shown by Figure 8b which produces an after-image of a different color from the same green. This is color adaptation—the hues and saturations of perceived colors depend on the color adaptation state of the eye.

The eye also adapts to brightness, and it is this adaptation that is largely responsible for the perception of gray and black. If a dim area of light is placed on the screen as an isolated color, you will see just a dim

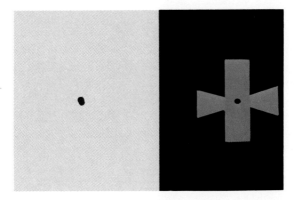

Figure 8a

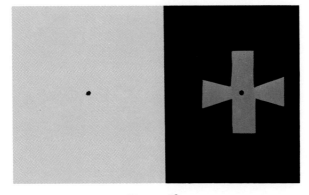

Figure 8b

area of light. If enough time passes and the room is dark, this light eventually seems quite bright. If this area is surrounded with the light from the projector, it appears black. This is because the eye's adaptation level has been raised suddenly by this surrounding, and the stimulus seen before as dim is now seen as black. This is the way gray and black are produced—by the relationship of the stimulus to its surround. It is not wrong to say that the gray and the black are produced by the surround and not by the stimulus itself although, of course, the stimulus determines how much gray is seen. In other words, gray does not have any single, simple physical counterpart in the stimulus. It is caused by the interaction in the mind of the relationship of the stimulus to its surround. Gray is not a physical entity, or object, however much it may appear so. A flat gray object, lighted separately in a dark room, appears white.

The addition of gray to a stimulus is a continuous process. That is, by changing the relation of the stimulus to the background the amount of gray can be changed continuously. By increasing the amount of gray steadily we arrive at black which is the limiting case of gray.

If we surround a dim spot of light with a lighter border, the center appears gray; if we do this again, we produce two shades of gray and a border which appears white. If another brighter border is added, we produce three shades of gray with a dark center. Each gray area has been determined by its brightness with respect to the brightest border. This process continues until the center appears black.

Figure 9a shows one more border. The first spot mentioned which went black with the surround had a brightness of only 1/100th of that of the surround. The center spot here is only 1/20th and hence does not

Figure 9a

look as black. This induction of gray, as it is called, has been shown for achromatic light with neither hue nor saturation. The same thing occurs with colors that do have hue and saturation. Figure 9b is included to help the reader visualize such a situation. Here, of course, the outer border seems gray because of the white paper. When we say that two colors differ in their content, we mean that the outside border contains zero gray, and the inside border has a greater gray content than the one between them. Sometimes adding gray to colors in this way changes the

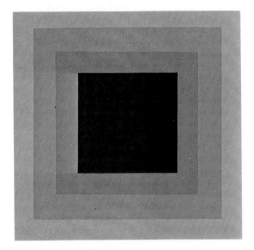

Figure 9b

character of the color so much that we give it a new name. For example, a reddish-orange surround by white appears to become brown. We are so familiar with brown that it is difficult to see that it is simply the previous color with gray added. Sometimes the addition of gray produces a shift in hue. For example, when a distinctly reddish purple is surrounded by white, it appears distinctly blue-purple.

What in the stimulus determines how much gray will be added to it by a given surround? In other words, what is the relationship of a color to its surround that determines the amount of gray that will be seen? Newhall, Burnham, and I studied this extensively some years ago with surprising results. Figure 10a is a photograph of a page of the Munsell "Book of Color." It represents all the chips in the system that have the single hue 5 red. At the left are the achromatic grays, and as we proceed to the right, saturation increases in all the rows to the maximum they could attain with permanent pigments. (No attempt has been made at an exact reproduction.) Vertically the gray scale is placed in equal visual

Figure 10a

steps, and all the colors in any horizontal row have the same reflectance as the gray step of that row. Starting at the top of any vertical row and looking down along that row, the gray content increases continuously to the bottom; it would reach black somewhere below the last chip. Correspondingly, if we look at the gray step in any horizontal row and follow that row to the right, the gray content of the chips decreases from this gray, and the gray would disappear just beyond the last chip in some of the rows. Since gray increases downward and decreases to the right, it is apparent that along some diagonal line down and to the right will be a series of colors that have the same gray content.

Not all of these colors can be produced with permanent pigments on paper, but they can be produced easily optically in the laboratory. Not only can we produce the zero gray colors, but we can go beyond them (to the right) to still higher saturations. To our surprise, all colors to the right of the top line appear fluorescent.

We are all familiar with the brilliant oranges and reds of safety belts, hunting jackets, posters, etc., that seem to glow with their own light. What we found was that it is not necessary for the color to actually be fluorescent to appear that way. It only has to lie to the right of the upper line.

Figure 10b shows a new line cutting across the others and sloping upward from left to right. At the lower left end of this line is a dark gray. As we progress along this line, gray decreases continuously until we come to zero gray. As we continue along this line, apparent fluorescence starts and increases continuously until we reach the line corresponding to the reflectance of white paper. Slightly beyond this line apparent fluorescence ceases, and the color takes on the appearance of a light source.

Two surprises were involved in these results. First, the appearance of fluorescence has nothing to do with actual physical fluorescence but only with the relationship of the color to its surround; secondly, fluorescent colors must have equal to or less reflectance than white paper if they are to appear fluorescent. Because of the continuous nature of the change from gray to fluorescent, no fluorescent color can contain gray, and it is legitimate to consider this phenomenon as negative gray content. I believe they are produced by the same visual mechanism, and I consider both as a single visual variable. Hence, the fourth variable following hue, saturation, and brightness is gray content or apparent fluorescence.

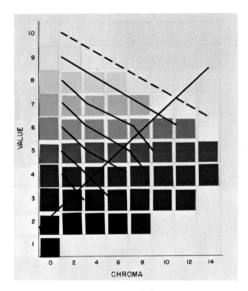

Figure 10b

Perception

Until now we have been considering the colors that we see. We now must take into account the way in which we see them. The distinction is important and seems to be too little understood.

If you are present in a natural scene such as shown in Figure 11a, you are perceiving color in three different ways. It is easy to become conscious of each of these in turn although, of course, seeing is usually an unconscious process. If the sun is shining, you see the sun as a light source. At night the light source may be an incandescent light bulb and so on. In any ordinary visual situation you can see or infer a light source. This is the first way of seeing color.

Light sources have the variables of an isolated color. They differ only in hue, saturation, and brightness and cannot appear gray and still appear as a light source. The second way of seeing color is to see it as the color of the light from the light source falling on objects. In Figure 11b, for example, light is falling on the objects, and this perception of

Figure 11a

Figure 11b

Figure 12a

Figure 12b

light illuminating objects is the most common experience of our visual lives. We cannot see objects at all unless they are being illuminated by something, and we take this illumination for granted. However, we can and do see this illumination as separate from the objects (Figure 12a). This perception of the illumination as distinct from the objects is one of the most vital facts of color vision. The illumination becomes the reference by which we judge the properties of the objects we see.

It is largely true that illumination sets our adaptation level—*i.e.*, it tends to set the sensitivity level of our eyes. In interpreting the scene in front of us, our ability to see this illumination as separate from the objects allows us to see what the object properties are. The possible color differences visible in illumination—and it can be colored, of course, as in stage lighting—include hue, saturation, and brightness but also gray because shadows are seen as part of the illumination, and they are seen as gray (Figure 12b).

The third way of seeing color in addition to light source and illumination is seeing it as the effect of the objects on the color of the illumination. Thus, the light falling on an object is of one color or, more usually, is colorless, and the light reflected from the object is of a different color. The perception, however, is a direct one, and rather than seeing this change of illumination color as an effect we actually see it as a property of the object. The third way of seeing color, then, is to see it as a property of an object. Since an object may change its color when placed under a different light source, we have to add that it is the color of the object that we are seeing at the moment.

We see object colors in Figure 12b, and objects which are more colorful are shown in Figure 13a. Light sources can vary in brightness and so can the illumination. The object color, however, cannot vary in brightness. Brightness is never seen as a property of an object; it is always seen as the property of the illumination or the light source.

Figure 13a

The property of objects that is seen and which is somewhat similar to brightness is called lightness. A color can be seen as lighter or darker than another, and the concept is the same as that in general speech. It is, however, always with respect to something else. If the something else is specified carefully, it is even possible to refer to the perception as that of relative brightness, but the perception is not the same as brightness, and it is better to call it lightness.

Lightness is the fifth variable, the only other perceptual variable of color as defined. Lightness is seen not only as a property of objects but also as a property of illumination to which we refer when we speak of a dark or a light shadow. With colors of moderate saturation and a considerable range in lightness, the concept of lightness is fairly simple. The objects in Figure 13b are good examples, and there is little difficulty arranging them in the order of their lightness. For colors of high satura-

Figure 13b

tion, however, there is little agreement among observers. For this reason measured luminous reflectance was used for this variable in the Munsell system. The objects in Figure 14a, however, would be much more difficult to arrange in the order of their lightnesses.

When a color appears fluorescent and lighter than white or when the color is seen against a black background and is obviously lighter than the background, the concept becomes quite confusing. This is an unre-

Figure 14a

solved problem. I have suggested that the word brilliance be used for the fluorescent colors lying beyond zero gray because it seems more logical than lightness, but there are objections to this. In any case, lightness or its equivalent is a necessary concept because it is one phase of what is seen, however defined. If words such as lighter, darker, more brilliant, duller, etc. express what is seen, they are satisfactory. Only when an attempt is made to systematize the perceptual variables and arrange all perceptions along some specified coordinates is any real difficulty encountered. That lightness is a real and necessary variable is shown by the fact that a series of colors of constant hue but containing no gray get darker as saturation is increased. That is, for colors not containing gray three variables are still necessary to describe them.

The systematization of lightness as a variable, however, in my opinion, has so far been accomplished only partially and only for a white or light gray background. At this point I disagree with the usual textbooks, including two of my own, because I now believe that lightness and gray content may be made to vary independently of each other. If we have a collection of colored areas on a white background as shown in Figure 14b, there is a fixed relationship between gray content and lightness that varies with hue and saturation; thus, if you specify hue, saturation, and lightness or gray content, you have specified the fourth variable. This is the basis of the Munsell system and essentially all others. With the background specified as white or any other color (just so that it is specified), we fix the relationship of gray content and lightness. All such colors can then be arranged in a three-dimensional space. It has been assumed that points in this space represent all possible color perceptions. I no longer believe this is true. These points do, to be sure, represent all the possible perception of colors seen against a white background, but it has been assumed that the effect of putting a color chip on some other background, say black, was simply to move the perception to another point in the same three-dimensional space. I believe that putting the chip on black moves it completely out of the space representing colors on white into the space for colors on black and that this space contains different colors—not differently located, but different colors.

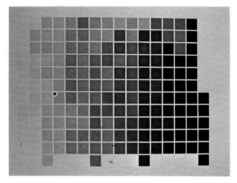

Figure 14b

Placing a color on black changes the relationship between lightness and gray content so that it is no longer represented. For example, if a color chip from Munsell 5 red at value 3 and chroma 4 is put on black velvet and illuminated with a lot of light, the saturation of the chip will increase, and its lightness will increase.

Munsell 5 red does not change its hue much on black so that the 5 red matches the chip for hue. The increase in saturation is represented also on the book page, but in the column of chips that has this saturation there are no chips that look like the one on black. The relationship of gray to lightness of the chip on black is not represented on the book page. Thus, I believe that it is not possible to produce a color on black which exactly matches one on white. I think artists have known this, at least intuitively, for centuries and have been puzzled by our insistence that it is not so.

Hence, it takes four dimensions to represent all object color perceptions, and it takes a series of three-dimensional spaces to illustrate them, not just one.

Summary

Five basic differences can be seen between colors. For light sources and isolated colors there are three—hue, saturation, and brightness; for object colors there are four—hue, saturation, gray content, and lightness; for illumination, there are all five.

How is it possible for there to be five color perception variables when it takes only three variables to match any color? The answer is that this statement is not applicable to perceived color. It is *not* possible to match any color perception by using only three variables. However, an *unrelated* color can be matched by using three variables, and this is the source of the belief. When an unrelated color is surrounded by another color (*e.g.*, a red dot on white paper), it takes three more variables to match this border, and we now have six variables, not three.

Suppose I want to show the red dot on black or dark gray or any other dark color. To show black I have to surround the whole by a brighter border. This means three more variables, and now we have nine. It takes nine variables generally to produce the perception of a color on black or on any color containing gray.

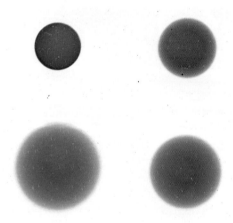

Figure 15a

Expressed somewhat differently, any color stimulus can be matched by using three properly chosen psychophysical variables, but it is not possible to produce all color perceptions with only three—generally it can take nine.

I am surprised not to have found more than five perceptual variables with nine in the stimulus. If there are only five, however, it is because the perceptions of hue and saturation are the same perceptions in all cases while the other three are intensity variables.

We began by restricting the definition of color to that of perfectly uniform areas in which we could see no color differences, and in practice this is a necessary restriction. It applies to everything we have said. If an exception is made for one particular kind of unevenness, however, we arrive at what appears to be an entirely new class of colors. For one hue and saturation such a color is seen in Figure 15a.

The color in the center of the dot on the lower left is physically identical to the one above it in the upper left. They differ in the fact that the upper one has a distinct edge while the lower one has a diffuse edge. The other two have edges that are intermediate. All four are identical at their centers. Similar dots of a different color are shown in Figure 15b.

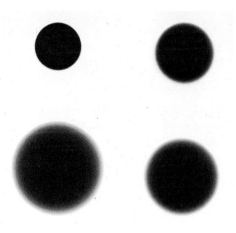

Figure 15b

The entire character of the color of the diffuse dot is different from that of the dot with the distinct edge. The diffuse-edge dot has a filmy, translucent quality which makes the sharp-edged dot seem hard by comparison. Such colors have been known to scientists for over 100 years, but I know of no investigation of them.

If we were to produce all possible colors on all possible backgrounds using only areas with distinct edges, would colors of the type seen in the lower left be included? I am inclined to think that they would not, but I shall leave the matter there. In any case I am sure that this effect is the cause of the glowing beauty of the colors in the background of Figure 16a where the out-of-focus color areas have this quality. Such colors are seen again in the background of Figure 16b.

Figure 16a   Figure 16b

Color is not a simple subject, and there may be some who regret this. However, the very complexity of color and the way we see it is responsible for the wonderful variety and occasional great beauty of the colors we see in the world around us. For this reason we should be thankful that the subject is, in fact, so complicated.

Color-Difference Evaluation

DAVID L. MAC ADAM

Research Laboratories, Eastman Kodak Co., Rochester, N. Y. 14650

Normal color vision is so acute that only the most accurate instruments and methods are adequate for color measurement and evaluation against tolerances. The basic instrument is the spectrophotometer. The evaluation procedure uses data provided by the International Commission on Illumination, supplemented by data concerning the color-difference sensitivity of people with normal color vision. Newly developed formulas facilitate the use of those data and make feasible the calculation of hue according to color geodesics, as proposed in 1920 by Erwin Schrodinger.

A system of colorimetry and color specifications was recommended in 1931 by the International Commission on Illumination (CIE) and has been standardized by the U. S. Standards Institution. Utopia for a colorist would be where the CIE X, Y, and Z values of a production sample always come out exactly equal to the values for the standard, but in the real world they never do. This means we never get an exact color match, and we must agree on tolerances. It is practically impossible to express tolerances in terms of X, Y, and Z, so we have to look into the matter further.

For many purposes, slight errors of lightness are not as serious as equally small errors of color quality—*i.e.*, hue and saturation, or chroma, or call it what you will. In any event, the tolerances for lightness depend in a different way on the conditions of examination and use than do tolerances of color quality.

The X, Y, Z system was designed with this in mind. The curves are such as to make it easy to separate lightness from color quality. Lightness is measured and expressed as luminous reflectance, which is indicated simply by the second tristimulus value, Y. If a sample has a lower value of Y than the standard, the sample looks darker. Color quality is a more complicated matter.

Chromaticity Diagram—A Map of Color Quality

The CIE chromaticity diagram is so important that some of its features warrant discussion. I like to think of it as a map of color quality. We use x like longitude (west to east) and y like latitude (south to north). Figure 1 shows such a map. White and gray are in the middle. Remember, this is a map of color quality only. The amount of color, or luminous reflectance, is not shown. Just as the heights of hills are written on a road map, if one wishes to indicate the luminous reflectance of a color here, a number must be written on the map, beside the point representing the color quality.

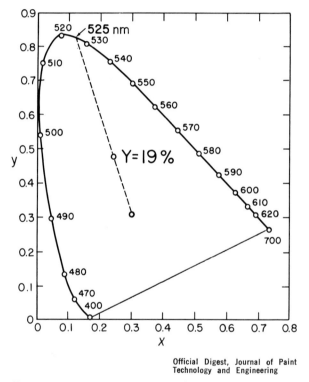

Official Digest, Journal of Paint
Technology and Engineering

*Figure 1. Determination of dominant wavelength
and purity on CIE chromaticity diagram (x,y) (8)*

The spade-shaped outline represents the most vivid colors, which are the colors of the spectrum. It encompasses all real colors. You can't make any colors corresponding to places outside the spectrum boundary. As a matter of practical fact, you can't even make any that would be represented by points close to the upper or left portions of that boundary. For example, Figure 2 shows the range of colors that can be produced by using the best modern printing inks. This range is shown, as actually printed with such inks, in *Scientific American* (*13*). A similar illustration, exhibiting practically the same range of colors was printed nearly 25 years ago in *Life* (*4*). It was reprinted in the *Journal of the Optical*

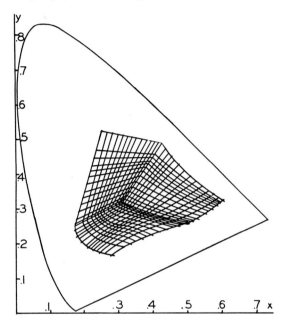

Figure 2.   Gamut on CIE chromaticity diagram of colors that can be produced by printing inks. Each boundary curve within the gamut is the locus of a constant amount of one of the inks. The upper right boundary has the maximum concentration of the yellow ink. The left boundary, to the bottom corner, has the maximum concentration of the cyan (bluish green) ink. The lower right boundary has the maximum amount of the magenta (bluish-red) ink. Each ink has zero concentration at the triple point in the center and along nearly straight loci that radiate from it, more or less parallel to the corresponding boundary loci of maximum concentrations.

Society of America (*3*), which may be more readily accessible. The curved part of the boundary, at the left, represents the colors of the short-wave end of the spectrum (*see* Figures 1 or 3 for the wavelengths), from violet at the bottom through blue and bluish-green to green at the top. The nearly straight part of the boundary, towards the right, represents the long-wave colors, from green at the top through yellow and orange to red at the lower right corner. This much of the boundary of real colors, consisting of the left, upper, and right portions is called the spectrum locus. The straight line that closes the bottom is the boundary of the most saturated, or vivid, reds, red-purple, true purples, and purple-violets.

Dominant Wavelength. The closer a point is toward the center, the less vivid or saturated is the color it represents. Except for that, its hue is approximately the hue of the part of the spectrum represented by the intersection of the boundary curve with the straight line drawn through the color point from the white point. Therefore, we can specify the hue conveniently by drawing that line and determining the wavelength represented by the point where that line intersects the spectrum boundary.

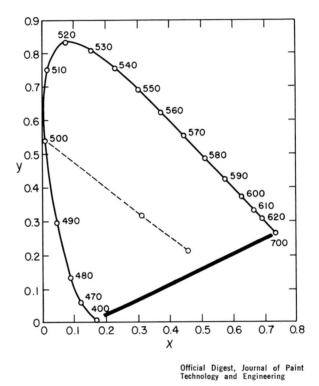

Official Digest, Journal of Paint
Technology and Engineering

Figure 3. Determination of complementary wavelength (8)

For the example shown in Figure 1 it is 525 mμ. This is called the dominant wavelength. It is not the highest point on the spectrophotometric curve. The only way we can find the dominant wavelength is by drawing the line, such as is shown in Figure 1, or by using charts on which the lines are already drawn, like the large ones printed in the "Handbook of Colorimetry" (1).

Complementary Wavelength. Of course, lines drawn from the white point through points in the lower portion of the map do not cut the spectrum boundary. The straight boundary of the purples does not represent colors found in the spectrum. To interpret colors represented by points in the lower portion of this map, we draw the line backwards, as in Figure 3, from the point representing the sample, up through the white point, until it cuts the spectrum-boundary curve. The wavelength where that line cuts the spectrum boundary is called the complementary wavelength of the purple.

Purity. For all cases the fractional distance of the sample point from the white point to the nearest boundary is called the purity of the color of the sample. It is usually expressed as percent. Although purity

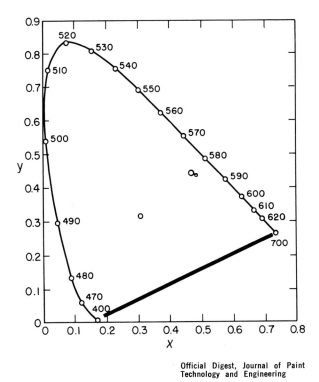

Figure 4.   Chromaticity locations of a standard yellow material (larger circle near 580 nm) and its red tolerance limit (8)

usually increases with increase of the subjective impression of saturation of colors of a given hue, when they are viewed under standard conditions, equality of purity does not usually assure equality of the subjective impressions of saturation of colors that differ in either hue or lightness (*i.e.*, luminous reflectance, *Y*). The slightest separation of points in any direction, in any region of the chromaticity diagram, represents a real color difference, which may be quite visible.

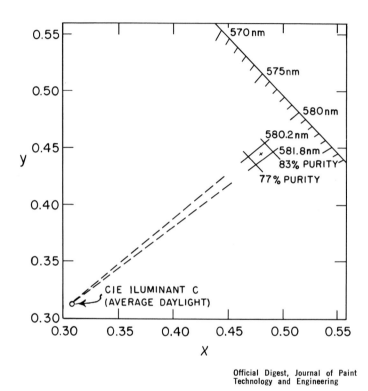

Official Digest, Journal of Paint
Technology and Engineering

Figure 5.   Tolerance boundaries and dominant wavelengths and purities of tolerances for variations from the standard yellow (x), *shown on enlargement of upper right section of chromaticity diagram* (8)

Color-Difference Evaluation

Returning to the color-difference evaluation problem, the basic question is "how close to a standard color is the point representing a production sample if they are barely satisfactorily matched"? The larger circle to the right in Figure 4 represents the standard for a certain long-established yellow material. The small adjacent circle represents the reddish-tolerance limit. Any samples represented by points farther than that from the standard point are too red. Carloads of material have been rejected as being too red on this basis.

Color Tolerances. These points are so close together that it is inconvenient and dangerous to work at this scale. Let's take the little area shown in Figure 5, magnify it and see where our standard yellow and tolerance limits are. In Figure 6 the point representing the standard is in the middle of the cluster; the reddish limit is at the lower right; the greenish limit is at the upper left; the high-purity, or strong, limit is at the upper right, and the low-purity or weak limit is at the lower left.

Remember how close together the points representing the standard and the reddish-tolerance limit were in the map of all color qualities. Because they are so close, color must be measured very accurately if the measured differences are to be reliable for evaluating visible color differences. Short cuts, "good enough" instruments, and carelessness are simply no good.

What about the sample that is strong and reddish but just barely within the corner (Figure 6) drawn through the limits, with sides parallel to the lines connecting the limits? This set of tolerances was set up 25

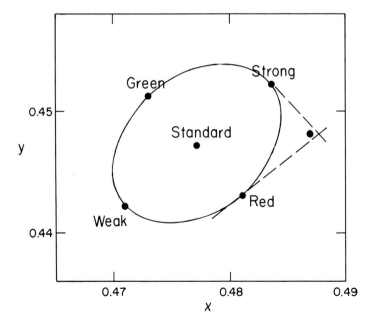

Official Digest, Journal of Paint
Technology and Engineering

Figure 6. Further enlargement of Figures 4 and 5, showing locus of colors all as acceptable as the red, green, weak, and strong tolerance limits. The color represented by the dot just inside the right corner of the quadrilateral tolerance diagram (transcribed from Figure 5) is not as acceptable as the four named tolerance samples (8).

years ago in terms of dominant-wavelength and purity limits; the limits were represented by the parallogram whose corner is sketched here. The old dominant-wavelength and purity specifications might be interpreted so as to accept such a sample, but we now know that its difference from the standard is visually about 40% greater than the difference between the standard and any of the four tolerance limits. For equal noticeability in such cases, the tolerance boundary should be an ellipse, which would, of course, exclude and dictate the rejection of that strong reddish sample. How about similar tolerances for other colors—green, blue, purple, red, orange, and even white, brown, and various pastels?

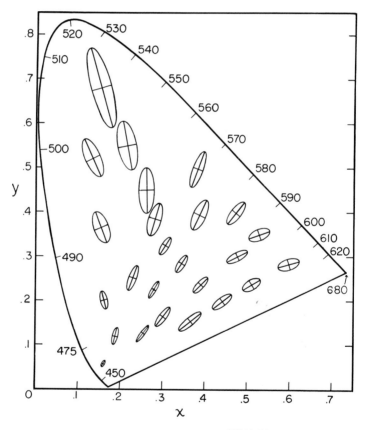

Official Digest, Journal of Paint
Technology and Engineering

Figure 7.   Twenty-five loci of colors, all 10 times as different from the aim colors (at the intersection of the axes of each ellipse) as the standard deviation of visual color matching when the observer has complete and convenient control over the matching color (on CIE (x,y) diagram) (8)

Color-Discrimination Ellipses. Some ellipses around various other colors are shown in Figure 7. However, these represent differences about 10 times as large as the tolerances shown by the ellipse in Figure 6. I had to expand these ellipses so we could examine them simultaneously.

The map of colors shown in Figure 8 was recommended by the CIE in 1960 as being more nearly representative of color differences. On it are drawn the color-discrimination ellipses (enlarged 10 times). The ratio of greatest to smallest radius is still about 4:1. That's better than nearly 30:1, which was the ratio in the old standard map, but it isn't satisfactory for critical tolerance work.

Computing Color Differences. Recently, I have used a high speed computer to establish a machine method for computing color differences, so that we can escape the temptation to use such crude graphical approximations.

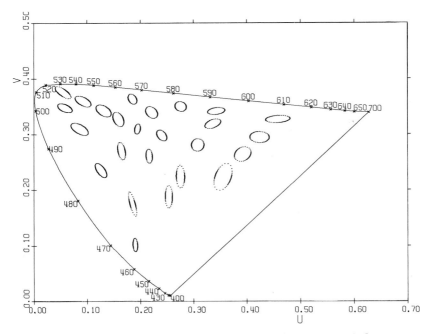

Figure 8. Ellipses from Figure 7, represented on CIE (u,v) diagram

If we wish, we can compute the x- and y-coordinates for the old CIE color map and use the new formula for color difference in terms of those coordinates. However, the formulas are simplest, and can even be used for hand calculation, if we use a different set of color-mixture functions, which are shown in Figure 9.

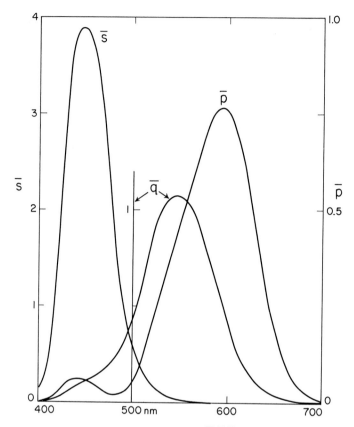

Figure 9. Color-mixture functions $\bar{p},\bar{q},\bar{s}$ *of optimum shapes for use in optimized, modified Friele 1965 formulas for color difference (Equations 1 and 2)*

These functions can be built into tristimulus integrators or they can be programmed easily. They are connected with the CIE standard functions, x, y, z by the formulas:

$$\bar{p} = 0.69\bar{x} + 0.364\bar{y} - 0.0934\bar{z}$$

$$\bar{q} = -0.457\bar{x} + 1.3046\bar{y} + 0.1215\bar{z}$$

$$\bar{s} = 0.8466\bar{z}$$

These formulas for $\bar{p}$, $\bar{q}$, and $\bar{s}$ give results different from, but proportional to, those given by the formulas for R, G, B recommended by the Technical Committee on Colorimetry E-1.3.1 of the International Commission on Illumination (*14*). The formulas for $\bar{q}$ and $\bar{s}$ are normalized to give equal Q and S values—e.g., 100, for a perfect diffuse reflector (reflectance = 100) in CIE source C illumination. The value of P

for that case is 93, which is the optimized relation to use in the formulas for color difference.

The tristimulus values obtained by using the p, q, s transformation of the standard CIE tristimulus values X, Y, Z by use of the same formulas are called P, Q, S. To determine whether a sample is within tolerance, subtract the P value of the sample from the P value of the standard and call the result ΔP. Similarly, subtract the Q value of the sample from the standard Q value and call that result ΔQ; do the same for S and call that result ΔS.

Color-Difference Formula. The value of Δc given by the formula

$$\Delta c = [c_{11}(\Delta P)^2 + 2c_{12}\Delta P\Delta Q + c_{22}(\Delta Q)^2 +$$
$$2c_{23}\Delta Q\Delta S + c_{33}(\Delta S)^2 + 2c_{13}\Delta P\Delta S]^{1/2} \qquad (1)$$

tells whether the sample is within tolerance. For quite critical tolerances, Δc should be unity. For twice as big a tolerance (which will pass 8 times as many random samples), Δc should be set equal to 2.

Coefficients in Color-Difference Formula. The coefficient of $(\Delta P)^2$ in the color-difference formula is

$$c_{11} = [A(0.0778P^2 + Q^2) + T\,P^2S^2] \cdot K^2 \qquad (2a)$$

where

$$A = 57780\,[1 + 2.73\,P^2Q^2/(P^4 + Q^4)],$$
$$K = 1/(P^2 + Q^2),$$

and

$$T = 3228/(S^2 + .307\,Y^2).$$

Note that the CIE tristimulus value Y (*i.e.*, the luminous reflectance of the standard) is used in the formula for T. Here are the formulas for the other c's.

$$c_{12} = [(0.0778 - 1)\,APQ + TPQS^2] \cdot K^2, \qquad (2b)$$

$$c_{22} = [A\,(P^2 + 0.0778Q^2) + TQ^2S^2] \cdot N^2, \qquad (2c)$$

$$c_{13} = -TKPS,\ c_{23} = -TKQS,\ c_{33} = T \cdot \qquad (2d)$$

Gauging the CIE 1960 u,v Diagram. To show the relation of these formulas to the u,v diagram (Figure 8) recommended in 1960 by the CIE, the diagram was divided into many small triangles (Figure 10). Assuming that the vertices represented equiluminous colors ($Y = 50$), I used Equations 1 and 2 to compute the color differences corresponding to every side of every one of those triangles. They gave values of Δc that averaged about 50. An IBM 360 computer with a Calcomp plotter was programmed to draw triangles with sides whose lengths are proportional to those values for the corresponding color differences. The program assembled those triangles into strips corresponding to the horizontal strips in Figure 10. The resulting strips are shown in Figure 11. Their sides are not straight or parallel, nor can the strips be fitted together in a plane.

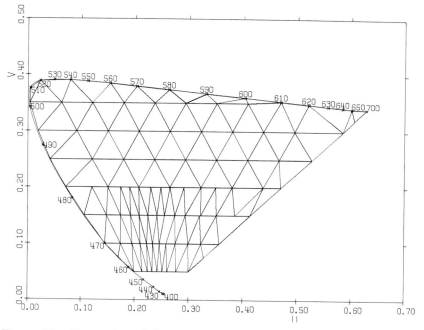

Figure 10.   Triangular subdivision of CIE (u,v) diagram, for test of color-difference formulas

Curved Color Surface. I previously assembled such strips to form a curved surface (5, 8, 9, 10). Such a surface can be produced by enlarging, cutting out the strips in Figure 11, and assembling them in proper order. The resulting surface has less severe curvatures than those shown in Refs. 5, 8, 9, and 10. However interesting that surface may be to geometers, such surfaces have not been usable in color technology; hence, even though it is less severely curved than previous versions, it is not shown here.

Optimized Plane Chromaticity Diagram. A plane diagram on which the corresponding triangle sides are most nearly equal to those shown in Figure 11 would have novel useful properties. Therefore, the program was modified so that the strips were drawn overlapping, as in Figure 12 so as to minimize the mean square distances between corresponding ver-

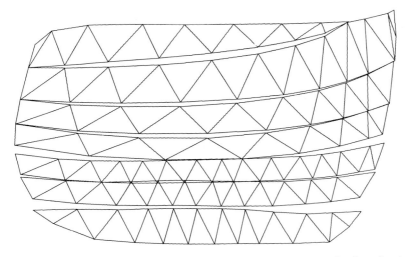

Figure 11. Triangles homologous to those in Figure 10. The length of each side of each of these triangles is proportional to the computed difference of the 2 colors represented by the ends of the corresponding side of the corresponding triangle in Figure 10. The strips corresponding to horizontal rows of triangles in Figure 10 cannot be put together without forcing them out of the plane.

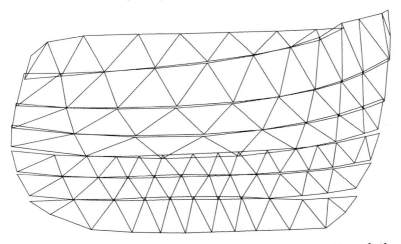

Figure 12. Partially overlapping plane strips from Figure 11, such that the mean-square error of coincidence of corresponding vertices is minimized. The horizontal and vertical coordinates of the vertices in this diagram were used with a linear-regression program to obtain Equation 3.

tices in adjacent strips. Simultaneously, rectangular coordinates ξ, η of all of the vertices, on a common set of axes with Δc units, were punched out. The x,y coordinates of the vertices of the original triangles (Figure 10) were also computed and punched out. A stepwise linear regression program was used to determine the most significant powers and cross products of x and y up to the fourth order (including a constant) to use in formulas for ξ and η. Subsequently, square roots and fourth roots of x and y and their products were also included. For the best fits, the standard deviations of reproduction of ξ and η were 13 and 2.4. I discovered that if I used powers, cross products, and roots of the CIE 1960 coordinates u,v, instead of x and y, the standard deviations were reduced to 10 and 2.16. Intrigued, I investigated what could be accomplished by varying the coefficients in the formulas for u,v in terms of x,y. The best results were obtained when different formulas for u and v were used to fit ξ rather than to fit η. Very little improvement of the fit for η resulted from including the square roots and fourth roots; hence they have been omitted.

Formulas for ξ,η Coordinates. For ξ, the best formulas found for u and v are:

$$u = x/(22y + 3.5x + 1)$$
$$v = y/(22y + 3.5x + 1)$$

With those values of u and v, the best formula for ξ is

$$\xi = 436581.2u^2 - 12464250u^4 - 625742v^2 + 11666943v^3 + 1942510uv -$$
$$17689035u^2v - 9658606uv^2 + 26321280u^3v - 19422\sqrt{u} +$$
$$5965.7\sqrt[4]{u} - 200. \tag{3a}$$

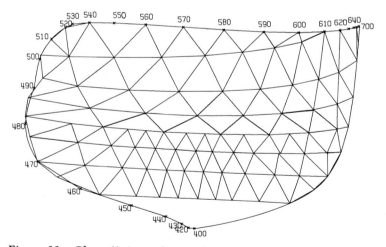

Figure 13. Plane (ξ,η), nonlinear chromaticity diagram, showing triangles homologous to those in Figure 10, whose sides are nearly proportional to the corresponding color differences according to Equations 1 and 2

For η, the best formulas found for u and v are:

$$u = x/(3.33y - 0.4x + 1)$$
$$v = y/(3.33y - 0.4x + 1),$$

in terms of which

$$\eta = 1996v - 12141v^2 + 32628v^3 - 376u + 1815u^3 - 2368u^4 -$$
$$5538uv^2 + 7805u^2v - 36052u^2v^2 + 77466uv^3 + 30. \qquad (3b)$$

The root-mean-square (rms) error of reproduction of the ζ coordinate of the vertices of the individual triangles in Figure 12 is 5.66. The rms error of reproduction of the η coordinates is 2.11.

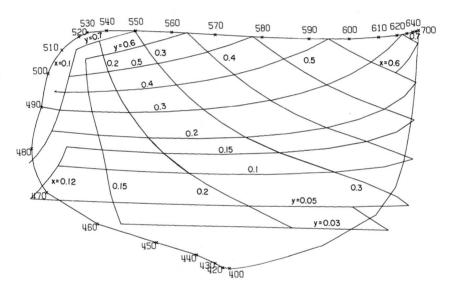

Figure 14.   *Loci of constant values of CIE* x,y *coordinates, in the* ξ,η *diagram*

The triangles corresponding to those in Figure 10, as reproduced by these formulas, are shown in Figure 13. Selected loci of constant x and y in the ξ,η diagram are shown in Figure 14. The ellipses corresponding to the original observer's data are shown in Figure 15, which may be compared with Figures 7 and 8.

Geodesic Constant-Hue Loci. In 1920 Schrodinger (*12*) suggested that geodesics based on such data, drawn from the point representing white should be loci of constant subjective hue. Conceivably, Equations 1 and 2 could be used to compute geodesics, but several attempts have failed because the algebra becomes so formidable. Figure 14 offers an attractive, simple alternative. If all the corresponding vertices in Figure 12 coincided, all straight lines drawn in the ξ,η diagram (Figure 14) would be geodesics. Therefore, straight lines drawn from the point representing white in the ξ,η diagram would be loci of constant hue according to Schrodinger's hypothesis. I have used the ξ,η and x,y coordinates of the vertices in Figure 12 and the stepwise regression program to obtain formulas for x and y in terms of ξ and η. Because their rms errors are great—0.0028 and 0.0045 respectively—I am reluctant to publish them, but I have used them to compute the x,y coordinates of a number of points on straight lines radiating from the white point in the ξ,η diagram.

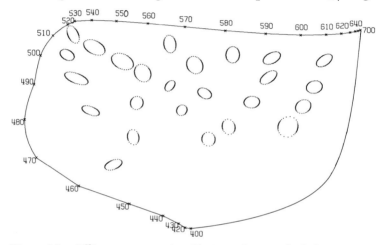

Figure 15.   Ellipses representing 10 times the standard deviations
of color matching in the ξ,η diagram

Curves connecting those points are shown in Figure 16. These are quite similar to subjectively determined constant hue loci of the Munsell Renotations (*11*) and to curves obtained by stretching a thread (*6, 7*) around a curved surface constructed by assembling strips similar to those in Figure 11.

Conclusions

Apart from their own interest, the constant-hue curves shown in Figure 16 indicate the validity of the ξ,η diagram and justify the use of Equation 3 for evaluating chromaticity differences.

To evaluate the noticeability of a chromaticity difference, simply compute ξ_0,η_0 from the CIE x,y coordinates of the comparison color; similarly compute ξ,η for the test color. The chromaticity difference Δc is then simply the distance

$$\Delta c = \sqrt{(\xi - \xi_0)^2 + (\eta - \eta_0)^2} \qquad (4)$$

The contribution of any luminance difference, $\Delta Y = Y - Y_o$, can be in-

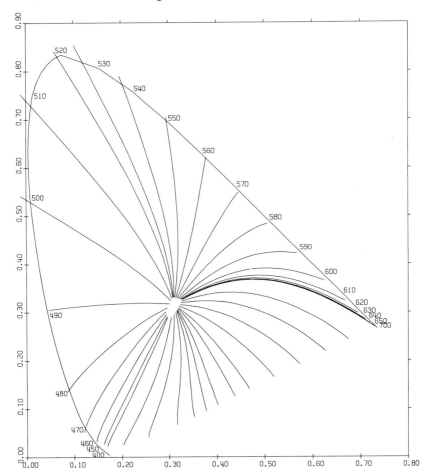

Figure 16. Loci of constant hue, according to the Schrodinger hypothesis, transformed from straight lines drawn outward from white (Illuminant C) in Figure 13

cluded by adding a term $(K\Delta Y/Y)^2$ inside the square-root sign. The coefficient K, appropriate for each application, should be determined by a few trials. It is subject to wide variations and may be a function of Y. Use of Equations 3 and 4 in this manner is much simpler than use of Equations 1 and 2.

Literature Cited

(1) Hardy, A. C. *et al.*, "Handbook of Colorimetry," Technology Press, Cambridge, Mass., 1936.
(2) Jones, L. A. *et al.*, "The Science of Color," Crowell, New York, 1953. Available from the Optical Society of America, 2100 Pennsylvania Ave., Washington, D. C. 20037.

(3) *J. Opt. Soc. Am.* **1945,** 35, 294f.
(4) *Life* **July 3, 1944.**
(5) MacAdam, D. L., *J. Franklin Inst.* **1944,** 238, 195.
(6) MacAdam, D. L., *Rev. Optique* **1949,** 28, 161.
(7) MacAdam, D. L., *Doc. Ophthalmol.* **1949,** 3, 214.
(8) MacAdam, D. L., *Offic. Dig., J. Paint Technol. Eng.* **1965,** 37, 1487.
(9) MacAdam, D. L., *J. Phot. Sci.* **1966,** 14, 229.
(10) MacAdam, D. L., *Phys. Today* **1967,** 20, 27.
(11) Newhall, S. M., Nickerson, D., Judd, D. B., *J. Opt. Soc. Am.* **1943,** 33, 385.
(12) Schrodinger, E., *Ann. Phys.* **1920,** 63, 418, 481.
(13) *Sci. Am.* **Sept. 1968.**
(14) Wyszecki, G., *J. Opt. Soc. Am.* **1968,** 58, 291.

RECEIVED June 6, 1969.

Calculations for Colorant Formulations

EUGENE ALLEN

Center for Surface and Coatings Research, Lehigh University,
Bethlehem, Pa. 18015

*To match a shade by calculation from its reflectance curve,
we must be able to relate reflectances to colorant concentrations. To do this, we use the Kubelka-Munk law. The
simplest application of this theory assumes that the reflecting
material is thick enough to be opaque and also that the
addition of colorant does not change the scattering properties of the substrate. These assumptions hold in general for
textile fibers and for pastel shades of paint. Based on this
theory, computer programs have been written for determining the best possible formulas to match a given shade.
Successively more difficult applications of the basic theory
are to dark shades in paints, semi-transparent paint films,
and printing inks.*

The science of colorimetry has passed through two clearly defined
phases. Each was of great technological importance, enabling ma-
chines to handle tasks which previously could be done only by experienced men. Both phases represent an emancipation from routine visual
methods.

In the first phase, we were freed gradually from the offices of the
color inspector—the individual who decided which lot of production
could be shipped and which would have to be reworked. With the
advent of the standard CIE system in 1931 and the development of
suitable color measuring instruments, this tedious job was supplanted
by instrumental methods. Quality control charts, based on measured
color variables, also made possible the detection of incipient drifts away
from the standard color in the manufacturing process.

In the second phase, we are gradually being freed from the offices
of the color matcher, whose function it is to obtain a formula for repro-
ducing any desired color on a given substrate. The color matcher is
much more skilled than the color inspector since he not only must be
able to detect color variations but also must know what to do about

them. In the same way the science of color matching is much more complicated than that of color specification since it is based on the latter but goes much further. In fact, not much could be done in color matching until computers became available. Nevertheless, it will never be possible to replace the color matcher, who is really an artist in his field. It will be possible only to free him from the routine duties of his office to concentrate on the more difficult problems he is constantly facing. In two previous papers I have tried to give some insight into just what a color matcher does (2, 3).

This paper discusses some current theoretical and commercial aspects of computer colorant formulation. This phase of color science is very new and is developing rapidly. For reasons below, textile dyeing and the coloration of paper and plastics in bulk were the first fields in which scientific color formulation was used because they are also the easiest fields as far as theory is concerned. Equally simple and almost as quick to mature was the formulation of paints in pastel shades (those containing a large amount of white pigment). Next in order of difficulty was the formulation of paints in dark shades, and this is evolving today. The requisite theory has been worked out, and most of what remains is only a matter of programming computers and overcoming inertia. The one major field which remains to be studied is that of color printing on paper. We have begun some work on this problem in our laboratory.

Let us examine some of the fundamental theory on which color formulation is based so that we can understand why it is so much more difficult to match a paint in dark shades than in pastel shades.

Turbid Medium Theory

Color can be specified in terms of a reflectance curve, which gives the fraction of light reflected from a sample as a function of wavelength. For computational purposes, it has become customary (in Phase I of colorimetry as well as Phase II) to divide the reflectance curve up by taking values at every 10, or sometimes 20, nanometers. Consider one of these wavelengths—i.e., 420 nm. A certain sample of dyed fabric may have a reflectance value of 55% at this wavelength.

Now the color of this sample was achieved by adding dye to the uncolored fabric. A certain concentration of dye in the fabric was necessary to produce this reflectance value. If less dye had been added, the reflectance would have been higher because less light would have been absorbed; conversely, if more dye had been added, the reflectance would have been lower. The first thing to establish in color formulating is the relationship between concentration of colorant and reflectance value. Since the reflectance varies from wavelength to wavelength, a different quantitative relationship holds at each wavelength; however, the nature of the relationship is the same at each wavelength, and all that really changes is, in effect, a proportionality factor or factors.

If we were dealing with a colored solution instead of a reflecting surface, we would be on grounds much more familiar to the analytical chemist. He would immediately invoke the time-honored Beer-Bouguer Law:

$$A = \log_{10}(1/T) = ca \qquad (1)$$

where A is the optical density (absorbance) of the solution, T represents the fraction of light at the wavelength in question which is transmitted through the solution, c represents the concentration of colorant, and a is a proportionality constant which encompasses the length of the light path as well as the light-absorptive capacity of the colorant in question (the absorption coefficient). If more than one colorant is present,

$$A = \log_{10}(1/T) = \Sigma_i c_i a_i \qquad (2)$$

where i refers to the ith colorant in the solution. Thus, if we know the values of a, we can immediately calculate the transmittance of a solution containing any mixture of colorants. The Beer-Bouguer Law was derived from a differential equation which states that the loss of light in traversing an infinitesimal layer of solution is proportional to the intensity of the light striking the layer.

The case of the reflecting surface is more complicated than that of the clear solution. Such a surface is considered to be the front end of a film with strong light-scattering properties. In such a film, we must be concerned not only with an absorption coefficient but also with a scattering coefficient. The differential equations representing the fate of a light beam incident on such a film have been formulated and solved by several authors, but the treatment used most widely is that of Kubelka and Munk (*11, 12*) (the Kubelka-Munk theory). The following general equation represents the reflectance, at a specified wavelength, of any highly scattering film as a function of the absorption and scattering coefficients of the film and the reflectance of the background over which the film is placed:

$$R = \frac{1 - R_g(a - b \coth bSX)}{a - R_g + b \coth bSX} \qquad (3)$$

where R is the reflectance of a film of thickness X placed over a background of reflectance R_g, a is given by $1 + K/S$, b is given by $\sqrt{a^2 - 1}$, K represents the absorption coefficient, and S is the scattering coefficient of the film. Most surfaces are completely opaque, and this condition is expressed mathematically by allowing X to approach infinity in Equation 3. An "infinitely thick film" is one of such thickness that any increase in thickness does not affect its reflectance. It can be shown that as X approaches infinity, the reflectance of the film (denoted by the symbol R_∞) is given by Equation 4.

$$R_\infty = 1 + (K/S) - \sqrt{(K/S)^2 + 2\,(K/S)} \qquad (4)$$

This equation is more widely known in the form in which K/S, the ratio between the absorption and scattering coefficients, is expressed as a function of R_∞:

$$K/S = (1 - R_\infty)^2/2R_\infty \qquad (5)$$

The absorption and scattering coefficients, K and S, are each the sum of separate contributions from each of the colorants present:

$$K = K_o + \Sigma_i c_i k_i; \quad S = S_o + \Sigma_i c_i s_i \qquad (6)$$

where K_o and S_o represent the absorption and scattering coefficients of the substrate, and k_i and s_i are the absorption and scattering coefficients of unit concentration of component i.

However, if the scattering power of the substrate is much stronger than that of the colorants to be added, a considerable simplification is possible:

$$\frac{K}{S} = \frac{K_o + \Sigma_i c_i k_i}{S_o + \Sigma_i c_i s_i} \cong \frac{K_o + \Sigma_i c_i k_i}{S_o} = \rho_o + \Sigma_i c_i \,\rho_i \qquad (7)$$

where $\rho_o = K_o/S_o$ and $\rho_i = k_i/S_o$. Thus, for this type of system we have a situation similar to that in transmittance work (cf. Equation 2 and the last term in Equation 7). In both cases, some function of a measured spectrophotometric quantity is related linearly to concentration of colorants. This simple linearity allows a much more rapid calculation in formulation problems.

Application of Equations to Practical Problems

Let us now consider how these equations can be used in practical formulation work. We progress from the simplest to the most complicated cases.

Textiles. When a dye is added to a textile fiber, no marked change in the scattering properties of the fiber takes place. The dye is adsorbed onto the fiber and no longer exists as individual particles, except in certain special cases. All the scattering power is the property of the structure of the textile substrate. This is an almost ideal case for applying the condition expressed in Equation 7, and accordingly the dyeing of textiles represents the simplest application of color formulation techniques. It was therefore the first formulation problem to be solved.

To set up a system for color matching on textiles, the dyer must first prepare dyeings of all the dyes which may be of interest, at certain specified concentrations. He must then run reflectance curves of all these dyeings, and from these curves he would calculate K/S values using Equation 5, usually at every 20 nm. He would also run a reflectance curve of the undyed substrate. The K/S value obtained for the undyed substrate would be the ρ_o value of Equation 7. Knowing this, as well as the concentrations used for the dyeings, he can now calculate the ρ_i values for the individual dyes according to Equation 7. For example, to determine the ρ_i value for a certain dye at 420 nm, he would subtract ρ_o at 420 nm from the K/S value of the dyeing at 420 nm, and divide the resulting difference by the concentration of the dye used to prepare the dyeing. The ρ_i values for the other wavelengths for this dye, as well as the ρ_i values for all the other dyes at all the wavelengths, would be obtained in exactly the same way.

The dyer can now match a shade. Assume that he has received a paper sample, with a request to match the color of this sample with the dyes at his disposal on the particular fiber of interest. He would first measure the spectrophotometric reflectance curve of the sample to be matched and convert this to a series of K/S values. If he wishes to use a combination of three particular dyes to match the shade, the following set of simultaneous equations would apply:

$$c_1\,\rho_{1\cdot400} + c_2\,\rho_{2\cdot400} + c_3\,\rho_{3\cdot400} = (K/S)_{400} - \rho_{o\cdot400}$$
$$c_1\,\rho_{1\cdot420} + c_2\,\rho_{2\cdot420} + c_3\,\rho_{3\cdot420} = (K/S)_{420} - \rho_{o\cdot420} \qquad (8)$$
$$\cdots\cdots\cdots\cdots\cdots\cdots\cdots\cdots\cdots\cdots\cdots\cdots\cdots\cdots$$
$$c_1\,\rho_{1\cdot400} + c_2\,\rho_{2\cdot700} + c_3\,\rho_{3\cdot700} = (K/S)_{700} - \rho_{o\cdot700}$$

where $\rho_{1,400}$ represents the ρ_i value for dye 1 at wavelength 400 nm and similarly for the other ρ values; $\rho_{o,400}$ represents the ρ_o value for the undyed substrate at 400 nm; $(K/S)_{400}$ represents the K/S value of the sample to be matched at 400 nm; c_1, c_2, and c_3 represent the concentrations of the three dyes. These equations imply that the spectrophotometric curve is broken up into 20-nm intervals between 400 and 700 nanometers, and hence there would be 16 equations in the set given above. Since there are 16 equations with three unknowns, an exact solution is generally not possible. Several techniques have been evolved for obtaining workable solutions to these equations. All of them require computers of one sort or another.

A special-purpose computer called COMIC I (Kollmorgen Color Systems, Attleboro, Mass.) (8) attempts to balance the K/S values of the sample to be matched against a linear combination of K/S values of the dyes. The 16 K/S values of the sample are displayed on an oscilloscope screen as 16 dots outlining a curve. The concentrations are represented by knobs, which when turned to the proper values will succeed in straightening out the series of dots to produce a line across the screen. If an exact solution is not possible, a straight line will not be produced, but a rather jagged line will result, indicating that many of the equations are not satisfied; however, the line might be straight enough to indicate the solution would be fairly good and the match would hold quite well. By the residual irregularity in the curve, the dyer would be able to judge that one or another of the dyes that he has been using is not the right dye for the match in hand, and he would be able to judge what different dye to attempt.

If a straight line is not produced, COMIC I can be used to calculate a match to the tristimulus values of the standard. This will be a match only under the particular conditions (light source, field of view, etc.) used in the tristimulus calculation. It may or may not be a good match under some other condition, such as shifting from daylight to tungsten light. To perform this calculation, the operator must simultaneously zero three meters with the concentration knobs.

Many ways of solving these problems by digital computer are available. One of the simplest is to use regression analysis to get a least-squares fit to the K/S curve of the sample, the independent variables being the concentrations of the dyes (9, 13). Another, and more widely used, method is to match the tristimulus values of the sample under a specific light source, usually Source C. If the match is non-metameric, it will hold up under other light sources as well; this can be determined by color difference calculations under the secondary light cource. If three dyes are to be used in the matching mixture, a mathematical solution is always possible since there are three stimulus values to be matched under the primary light source. The necessary mathematics for calculating this kind of match has been worked out in detail, and several useful systems for industry have been described (1, 4, 5, 9, 10, 14). Powerful computing systems are now available in which the computer selects dye combinations from a list of possible dyes, these combinations giving superior matches regarding the absence of metamerism and low cost (2, 3).

Paper and Plastics. Transparent plastics are like solutions in their optical behavior, and accordingly, coloring problems are amenable to the simple approach of Equations 1 and 2. Opaque plastics and paper are like textiles in that almost all the light scattering is done by the substrate, and the procedure just described for textiles can be used.

Paints in Pastel Shades. Light-colored paints contain large amounts of white pigment and are shaded by small amounts of colored pigments. Because of the presence of a preponderance of white, the scattering coefficient can be considered to be essentially that of the white pigment, with a small contribution from the colored pigment. Accordingly, pastel paints can be formulated in the same way as textiles, and the procedure just described can be used practically *in toto*. However, the formula which interconverts K/S to reflectance must be modified because a refractive index discontinuity exists between the surface of the paint film and air. The nature of this modification has been considered by several workers (*15, 16, 17*). One formula recommended for this purpose (*7*) is:

$$R' = 0.04 + 0.384\ R/\ (1-0.6R)$$

where R' is the reflectance as measured by the spectrophotometer, and R is the reflectance which will be used in the theoretical calculations. This formula holds for the case where the film has a refractive index of 1.5.

Paints in Dark Shades. When the amount of white pigment in a paint is of the same order of magnitude as that of the colored pigments or when white is absent, we can no longer use the simpler equations described so far and must resort to Equation 6 which demands that K and S be calculated individually. The equations used are collectively referred to as the Kubelka-Munk two-constant theory, whereas the equations used for textiles are referred to as the Kubelka-Munk one-constant theory.

In setting up a color matching system of this type, the formulator must determine the K and S values for each of his colorants at each particular wavelength. Since he must determine two constants, he needs two separate drawdowns and must work simultaneous equations. If the paint is sufficiently translucent, he would measure the reflectance of a drawdown over both a black and a white background and would base his simultaneous equations upon Equations 3 and 6. However, if the paint is opaque so that the background cannot be discerned behind it, he would use a masstone and tint as his two drawdowns and would base his simultaneous equations upon Equations 4, 5, and 6. In many cases the same pigment is opaque at some wavelengths and translucent at others, and the technique may have to be changed partway across the spectrum. A detailed description of both the techniques and the mathematics required to solve this problem is available (*7*).

A special-purpose digital computer which has been programmed specifically to solve problems both in one-constant and in two-constant Kubelka-Munk theory has been devised. This computer, known as COMIC II, is similar to COMIC I in that it is designed for use specifically on color problems and has a convenient oscilloscopic display which gives the operator a feeling for what he is doing in terms of the spectrophotometric curve.

Printing Inks. This is by far the most difficult problem since in addition to the necessity for the two-constant theory we have added difficulties. The differential equations upon which the Kubelka-Munk theory is based assume complete homogeneity within the film. A printed sheet of paper is anything but a homogeneous film; it is, on the contrary, a highly structured material consisting of ink on the surface and partially penetrated and unpenetrated paper fibers underneath. Although work on this problem has been started in our laboratory at Lehigh University, no results are available as yet. Our approach is to use a multilayer model; the top layer consists of ink which has not penetrated the paper, the next lower layer is a mixture of ink and paper fibers, and the lowest layer contains paper fibers untouched by ink. Equation 3 is used for the bottom layer, the background reflectance being set equal to zero. Then Equation 3 is applied to the next higher layer, the background reflectance being set equal to the reflectance just calculated for the lowest layer. Finally, Equation 3 is applied to the topmost layer in the same way. A detailed description of the mathematics has been written (6).

Literature Cited

(1) Alderson, J. V., Atherton, E., Derbyshire, A. N., *J. Soc. Dyers Colourists* **1961,** 77, 657.
(2) Allen, E., *Am. Dyestuff Reptr.* **1965,** 54 (10) 57.
(3) Allen, E., *Color Eng.* **1965,** 3 (1) 15.
(4) Allen, E., *J. Opt. Soc. Am.* **1966,** 56, 1256.
(5) Allen, E., *Color Eng.* **1966,** 4 (4) 24.
(6) Allen, E., Paper presented at "Color 69," Stockholm.
(7) Davidson, H. R., Hemmendinger, H., *J. Opt. Soc. Am.* **1966,** 56, 1102.
(8) Davidson, H. R., Hemmendinger, H., Landry, J. L. R., *J. Soc. Dyers Colourists* **1963,** 79, 577.
(9) Gugerli, U., "SARFO, ein System der automatischen Rezept - Formulierung und - Optimalisierung," Vorabdruck eines Referates an der Internationalen Farbtagung Luzern 1965.
(10) Gugerli, U., *Textilveredlung* **1966,** 1 (1) 29.
(11) Kubelka, P., *J. Opt. Soc. Am.* **1948,** 38, 448.
(12) Kubelka, P., Munk, F., *Z. Tech. Physik* **1931,** 12, 593.
(13) McGinnis, P. H., Jr., *Color Eng.* **1967,** 5 (6) 22.
(14) Park, R. H., Stearns, E. I., *J. Opt. Soc. Am.* **1944,** 34, 112.
(15) Ryde, J. W., *Proc. Roy. Soc.* **1931,** A131, 451.
(16) Ryde, J. W., Cooper, B. S., *Proc. Roy. Soc.* **1931,** A131, 464.
(17) Saunderson, J. L., *J. Opt. Soc. Am.* **1942,** 32, 727.

RECEIVED June 6, 1969. Work supported by the Pennsylvania Science and Engineering Foundation and the National Printing Ink Research Institute.

Colorant Formulation and Color Control in the Textile Industry

ROLAND E. DERBY, JR.

The Derby Co., Inc., 49 Blanchard St., Lawrence, Mass. 01842

The development of instrumental color measurement and its application to color problems in the textile industry are reviewed. The areas considered are: color formulation, color control, color tolerances, standards, and color faults and their evaluation. In each of these areas a fairly detailed account is given of the capabilities of modern instrumentation and theory to deal with the problems. Many practical problems in the coloring of textiles lend themselves to instrumental solution. To realize the potential of these methods, we do not need an abundance of new theories but rather more precise and reliable instrumentation. Perhaps, more importantly, we need colorists thoroughly trained in the theory and practice of spectrophotometry, color measurement, and color science.

Color is often one of the most important feaures of a textile material. While many other physical, chemical, and mechanical properties are important in textile design, style and fashion dictate a major role for color. This article is concerned with textile color and the application of instrumental color measurement to some textile color problems.

A. C. Hardy's research at MIT from 1928 to 1935 resulted in the development of a recording spectrophotometer. This instrument, commercially developed by the General Electric Co., is used to measure the reflectance of a material rapidly and precisely. Hardy was so confident of the future for this type device that he stated in 1932 (15):

The utilization of color measurement is in its infancy . . . it seems inevitable that the control of color processes will be eventually taken over by men possessed of an accurate knowledge of the subject of color and equipped with suitable instruments.

During the decade 1935–1945 considerable research was devoted to the industrial development of Hardy's thesis. It is impossible to credit adequately those concerned since much of the significant work was not published, but Pineo and Stearns (American Cyanamid Laboratories), I. H. Godlove (General Aniline), Simon (Sidney Blumenthal), O'Neill (Pacific Mills), Hanlon (Mohawk Carpet Mills), and Ingle (Monsanto) come immediately to mind. In addition to their industrial experiments, basic studies were in progress at the National Bureau of Standards by Judd and Keegan, at the Department of Agriculture by Nickerson, and by Hardy and his outstanding staff at the MIT Color Measurement Laboratory. This latter group provided the nucleus for many contributors to the early efforts in this field. The classic "Handbook of Colorimetry" prepared under their direction was first published in 1936. Its concise, clear presentation of the essential facts has maintained the importance of this publication for over 30 years (4th printing, 1966).

Despite this substantial effort, which undoubtedly provided a better basic understanding of our problems, as late as 1954 the author could state (*12*):

Within the last ten years, progress has been made in instrumentation and techniques which should encourage the wide use of instrumental color control of textiles. That the practical realization of such programs is not widespread is evidenced by the fact that, to the author's knowledge, no more than ten spectrophotometers are actively engaged in such work in the United States. This is partly due to the high cost of the instrumentation and partly to the general feeling that such methods are complicated and of dubious practical value.

While reflectance or transmittance could be measured with considerable precision in a few minutes using the Hardy instrument, the resultant curve, plotting R (or T) as a function of wavelength was not interpreted readily in terms of visual results, particularly for small color differences. To relate two reflectance curves to the visual difference, one had to resort to the psychophysical theory of color measurement formalized by the CIE in 1931. This procedure has been well documented (*14*). Unfortunately, a fairly complicated integration is required. Although a few instruments were provided with mechanical or electrical integrators—the early MIT instrument had a prototype of a modern digital readout—most work had to be done by hand using a desk calculator. The results were slow, tedious, and often inaccurate. They were not suited to the routine use of statistical analysis since one rarely could afford two integrations. Thus, when Davidson and Imm produced their mechanical integrator in 1949 based on the Librascope "ball and disc" integrator, the way was open for much more widespread use of colorimetry as opposed to spectrophotometry. Note should be made here of R. S. Hunter's early work in carrying out the integration by carefully matching filter transmissions and photocell sensitivities. This early work provided the basis for all modern filter colorimeters.

In our laboratory, upon acquiring a Librascope, we became aware of the greater precision associated with continuous integration. In addition, multiple measurements within and between samples became commonplace. The application of simple statistical techniques to the data paid great dividends. In my opinion, we have not advanced greatly in the last 20 years over the basic instrumentation and techniques at our command in the late 1940's. The major gain has been in the area of more rapid data acquisition and the use of digital readout devices, which enable us to evaluate rapidly virtually any functional relation between the variables involved by high speed computers. These are conveniences and, in many cases, economic necessities, but they do not solve basic problems.

The major problems associated with textile color are:

(1) Color Formulation. The production of a formulation of colorants having the desired physical and chemical properties, which in addition produces the desired color (or shade) on the consumers' textile material.

(2) Color Control. Once the customer has accepted the above formulation and production is started, it is necessary to control the process variables to maintain and deliver the desired color.

(3) Color Tolerances. Inherent in the decision as to whether the process is in or out of control is the necessity for establishing tolerances.

(4) Standards. In many instances it is desirable to maintain "standard colors—*e.g.*, colors of military uniforms, insignia and flags, and historic emblems. Since physical samples may fade or change color with time, a method of specifying the color without retaining a sample is desirable.

(5) Color Faults and Their Evaluation. If, for any reason, a problem arises in producing the desired shade, formulation, fastness, etc., spectrophotometry and colorimetry (particularly the former) are useful tools in solving the problem.

We shall consider each of these problems in turn, confining most of our remarks to the problem of formulation.

Color Formulation

In the textile industry, color formulation generally implies "color matching." The color of an object poses no great difficulty to the average observer [for simplicity, we will restrict our discussion to object color (5, 17)]. Man's visual sense has developed to such a degree that color as an element of appearance is determined readily with considerable discrimination. As with many other phenomena in nature, a detailed quantitative comprehension of the entire process is not easily gained.

The study of atomic and molecular structure is a well known example of this type problem. Complex organic molecules contort, react, interchange atoms, etc., with little concern for those versed in the intricate mathematics of quantum mechanims to follow and explain their behavior; so it is with color and the eye.

Simply stated, color matching implies

$$\text{Color A} = \text{Color B} \tag{1}$$

The difficulty arises with the meaning of equals ($=$). It seems that what is implied is that the sensation of color is equal, or that

$$\text{Color Sensation A} = \text{Color Sensation B}$$

[In general, the statement should be Appearance A $=$ Appearance B where terms such as size, shape, location, texture, and gloss are considered. For this paper we will consider only the color aspect.]

The problem in color matching is: given Color A (Sensation A), how are the available variables adjusted to reproduce this visual response— on fabric, plastic, paper, or leather, for example. This is a very complicated problem for which no universally accepted solution can be given. Studies carried out over the last 200 years resulted in an important advance—*i.e.*, three suitably chosen variables are necessary generally to describe a color.

Recent important studies by Evans (*13*) on the variables of perceived color indicate that three variables may not be sufficient to describe color in the natural view—*i.e.*, surrounded by other colors.

It is not essential to our arguments that we commit ourselves as to the number of variables involved since the conclusions will be the same regardless of the choice of variables.

If for the sake of argument and simplicity we confine ourselves to the three variables—hue, saturation, and brightness (*5*)—a color may be related to the eye, brain, and related response systems.

$$\text{Color A} = (H, S, B)_a \tag{2}$$

This resultant visual sensation may, in turn, be related to many variables in the observer's environment or within his responsive system. Thus, the three variables may be related as follows (*5*):

$$(H, S, B) = f (E, R, r, g, b, M, S, A, O, T \ldots u, v, w) \tag{3}$$

Where the product of E and R represent the spectral composition of the light striking the eye, r, g, b the particular observer's spectral sensitivity, M his memory, (S) the nature of the surrounding, A the state of adaptation of the observer, (O) the nature of surrounding objects, (T), the observer's attitute and u, v, w, other unspecified variables. Thus, the color matcher's problem is to manipulate the variables at hand (dyes, concentrations, finishes, etc.) so that

$$\text{Color A} = (H, S, B)_A = \text{Color B} = (H, S, B)_A \tag{4}$$

Substituting the functional Equation 3 into this equality, one obtains a reasonably concise statement of the problem. Thus,

$$f\ (E, R, r, g, b, M, S, O, T \ldots u, v, w)_a \quad \text{must equal}$$

$$f\ (E, R, r, g, b, M, S, O, T \ldots u, v, w)_b$$

Since the color matcher is restricted in the number of variables he can control or manipulate, his dilemma under many practical situations is apparent.

Some basic facts need to be summarized at this point.

(1) Since the color of an object is a visual sensation, it is always related to the eye, brain, and related response systems.

(2) The general functional relationship in terms of the psychological scales, hue, saturation, and brightness is related in a fairly complicated and generally unknown way to the measurable variables.

Obviously, color cannot really be measured by any means other than the eye. However, by placing certain restrictions on the functional variables involved, it is possible to relate instrumental measurements to visual experience and, consequently, to obtain many useful results. That such a procedure is possible has been experimentally verified hundreds of thousands of times in the last few decades. How is this simplification carried out?

First, one eliminates all variables in Equation 3 except E, R, r, g, b, either by keeping them constant or by arranging conditions so they are zero. Next, recognize that under these restrictions only the reflectance (R) can affect the comparison of samples A and B by any one observer. Acknowledging this point, (E) and r, g, b, were standardized or defined in 1931. The result was the CIE system of color measurement, described in great detail elsewhere $(6, 14)$.

In this system,

$$\text{Color} = (X, Y, Z) = \int (E_{std}\ R, x, y, z) \tag{5}$$

or, keeping E_{std} and x, y, z, constant, we have:

$$\text{Color} = F\ (R) \tag{6}$$

Under the assumptions and restrictions imposed, we now have:

$$\text{Color A} = (X, Y, Z)_a = \text{Color B} = (X, Y, Z)_b \tag{7}$$

as the basic instrumental color measurement equation.

These results are implicitly related to the eye since

$f(x, y, z)$ (standard observer) = average of $f(r, g, b,)$ for n observers

With these fundamental considerations of instrumental color measurement in mind, we are prepared to consider the color matcher's request, "what dyes do I add and how much of each to match the customer's shade?" Since R (reflectance) is the only variable, for one observer examining the two samples under one light source—e.g., the standard observer in standard illuminant (C), it is clear that if $R_a = R_b$ then Color A will equal Color B (under the restrictions imposed above).

Part of the answer to the matching question then is to add dyes in the proper amount which have the spectral characteristics to produce identical reflectance for the standard and the match. One method of doing this (probably the only method guaranteeing success) has been detailed by Saltzman (26) as color matching by colorant identification. Often it is possible to obtain closely similar reflectances without resorting to identical colorants. The elegance of this approach is that the match will be independent of observer and illumination conditions provided the restrictions above are complied with.

How does one know that $R_a = R_b$? One determines $R_a = R_b$ by measuring the two samples on a spectrophotometer. Such a procedure may not be completely satisfactory since R in the preceding equations refers to the observer's illuminating and viewing conditions. These may be far different from those used in any particular instrument. The problems inherent in measuring R reliably have been treated in detail elsewhere (3, 16); hence, we shall not discuss them further here.

In using a spectrophotometer to measure the reflectance difference between two samples, it is usually hoped that since both samples were measured on the same instrument, the results will at least be comparative and proportional to the visual results. If there is any appreciable difference in texture between A and B, the experience is apt to be poor.

To proceed with the practical possibilities, let us assume that instrumentation is available that permits a reliable measure of R (actually, modern instruments produce satisfactory results in most cases if proper care is taken in sample preparation and presentation). A reliable reflectance measurement is defined as one which, when substituted in our functional relation for object color, produces results in agreement with the average observer under standard viewing conditions. A common method used by visual color matchers that approximates the use of a spectrophotometer is to examine the two samples under as many light sources as possible (north light, artificial daylight, tungsten light, fluorescent light, "overhand," etc.). If the samples match under all these conditions, the chances of the reflectances being significantly different are remote.

Often, owing to technical requirements other than color (*e.g.*, chemical stability, and cost), colorants must be used which cannot result in $R_a = R_b$. Under these circumstances, life becomes more difficult, but not impossible. Since the color, as seen by the observer, is an integrated result of the interaction of the light sources, reflectance and observer sensitivity (in the simple case), there are many combinations which fulfill the basic equation.

$$(X, Y, Z)_A = (X, Y, Z)_B \tag{8}$$

An example taken from practice is shown in Figure 1. This represents a compromise on the part of the color matcher necessitated by the fact that the available dyes for fiber B cannot possibly duplicate R_a. In general, these combinations are apt to be quite sensitive to the nature of the light source and to the observer. Such matches are called metameric or perhaps preferably conditional. They are a general source of complaints by customers regarding the quality of the match. The basic requirements for object color matches under the simplified color measurement conditions are summarized in Table I.

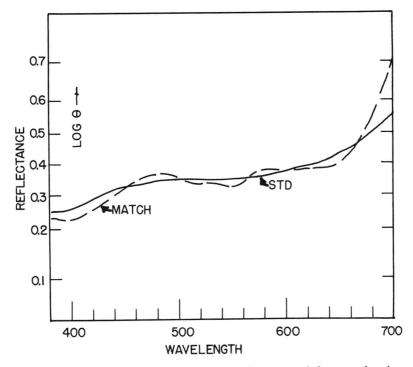

Figure 1.   A commercial metameric match prepared by visual color matching. Available colorants cannot match standard reflectance curve

Table I. Summary of Basic Color Matching Relations

(1) Color A = Color B when,

$$\int (E, R, r, g, b)_a = \int (E, R, r, g, b)$$

or, for instrumental color measurement purposes when,

$$(2) \quad (X, Y, Z)_a = (X, Y, Z)_b \quad \text{or,}$$

$$\int (E_{std}. R, \bar{x}, \bar{y}, \bar{z})_a = \int (E_{std}. R, \bar{x}, \bar{y}, \bar{z})_b$$

(3) A special case occurs when
$R_a = R_b$ (throughout the spectral range of visual sensitivity)
This match is independent of observer and illuminant.

(4) Generally, if

$$X_a = \int_{400 \text{ nm}}^{700 \text{ nm}} E_{std}. R_a \bar{x} \, d\lambda = \int_{400 \text{ nm}}^{700 \text{ nm}} E_{std}. R_b \bar{x} \, d\lambda = X_b$$

(similar expressions for Y, Z)

then, Color A = Color B under illuminant E_{std}, and to the observer x, y, z these may not correspond to any available light source or observer. This is a metameric or conditional match.

With hundreds of dyes at his disposal, how does the textile color matcher select the particular dyes and concentrations to satisfy the functional relations in Table I? Although extremely important technically, we shall not concern ourselves here with the methods of evaluating dyes for chemical and physical properties or fiber affinities. It is assumed that a range (20–30 dyes) is available displaying the requisite properties of chemical stability, cost, and ease of application. This assumption may be difficult to justify for a new synthetic fiber—e.g., polypropylene. Since little or no progress can be made unless we accept the availability of a suitable range of colorants, we will make this assumption. The question remains—how do we determine the quantity of the selected dyes necessary to obtain the desired values of R at different wavelengths?

This becomes complicated since the reflectance of a textile material, owing to scattering and surface reflection, is not a simple function of the molecular absorption characteristics of the applied dyes. In addition, the fiber has its own characteristic absorptions.

Much research during the last 50 years has produced a number of analytical and empirical relations of the form

$$C = f(R) \quad \text{or conversely} \tag{9}$$

$$R = F(C) \tag{10}$$

It is not sufficient merely to find a relationship that satisfies Equation 9. To be useful, it must be an additive function for each dye and substrate over the concentration range of interest, thus

$$f\ (R)\ _{total} = f\ (R)_{dye\ 1} + f\ (R)_{dye\ 2} + f\ (R)_f + \ldots \tag{11}$$

This important point was made by Parks and Stearns in a paper published in 1943 detailing the principles of instrumental color matching (*23*).

Illustrating such a function is the simple relationship that exists for solutions which follow Beer's Law, where the additive function relating concentration is

$$A = \log \frac{1}{T} = KC \tag{12}$$

Thus, for three dyes, one has the simple expression

$$A_{total} = A_1 + A_2 + A_3 \tag{13}$$

The mathematical details, assumptions, and boundary value solutions for the reflectance of turbid media have been extensively reviewed elsewhere (*17, 18, 19*).

With respect to colorant formulation on textiles, it is my opinion that sufficiently precise relationships are available to suit most needs, and little gain would be obtained in refining the present functional relations further, and generally increasing their complexity. This observation is not intended to discourage research work in this area for it is always better to understand the underlying reasons for physical observations.

It has been shown by several methods (*2, 18, 22*) that the function

$$\theta = \frac{(1 - R)^2}{2R} = KC \tag{14}$$

is a useful additive function for textile color formulation. This expression is equivalent to the Kubelka-Munk analysis for the reflection of turbid media having zero transmission. In their two constant theory, $\theta = K/S$ where K is an absorption coefficient and S is a scattering coefficient. Pineo (*25*) derived an identical expression independently without the necessary restrictions placed on the Kubelka-Munk analysis. For low values of R the surface reflection of the material R_s should be subtracted before applying Equation 14. R_s is generally less than 1%. In most textile applications K/S is taken as a ratio, with absolute values for either constant unknown, hence is more conveniently designated θ.

Since $\theta = KC$, this is an additive function, and we have

$$\theta_T = \theta_f + \theta_{D1} + \theta_{D2} + \theta_{D3} \tag{15}$$

for a three-dye (D_1, D_2, D_3) system plus substrate (θ_f).

Since Equation 14 relates concentration to reflectance, the condition $R_A = R_B$ will be satisfied if $\theta_A = \theta_B$.

In stating that $R_A = R_B$ we are referring to the complete visible spectrum (approximately 400–700 nm). Thus, when we indicate a match is obtained for $\theta_A = \theta_B$, the same range is indicated.

The "matching equations" in terms of dye concentrations, are then

$$\theta_A = \theta_B = C_1\,\theta_{D1}' + C_2\theta_{D2}' + C_3\,\theta_{D3}' \tag{16}$$

where θ_{D1}' is the value of $(1 - R)^2/2R$ for a known concentration of Dye_{D1}.

Colorants must be found whose spectral absorption characteristics are such that concentrations can be found to satisfy Equation 16 at all wavelengths. It is obvious that without a high speed computer or some special technique such a solution would be difficult to find. Some hint as to the solution may be obtained by noting that to match a blue we should not choose a brown dye: thus, by this logical procedure, the number of random trials can be reduced drastically.

An ingenious method of solving Equation 16 was patented in 1938 by Pineo (American Cyanamid Co.). It involves devising a system wherein a spectrophotometer plots the function $\log \theta$ as an ordinate instead of reflectance. By this method, curves as a function of wavelength are produced, whose shape (ratio of absorption to scattering as a function of wavelength) is independent of concentration. Changes in concentration merely displace the curves vertically as shown in Figure 2. For a solution to the matching equation at all wavelengths to be possible, it is necessary that some vertical displacement of the curves for individual dyes ($\log \theta_{dye\,1}$, etc.) permit superposition on the $\log \theta_a$ curve. If this appears possible, the concentrations may be obtained by solving three simultaneous equations or by the nomographical method developed by Stearns (27).

Figure 3 shows this procedure for a simple three-dye combination. The procedure has been discussed in considerable detail by Derby (10). While this method has existed for some time, it still has considerable utility in solving problems involving textile colorants.

For the last 20 years nearly all reflectance curves recorded in our laboratories have been drawn with $\log \theta$ as the ordinate. The utility of this type of presentation arises from its speed (55 sec), flexibility, and simplicity of interpretation. Simple formulations, containing two to three dyes, with clearly separated absorption maxima can be prepared in a few minutes. More complicated ones, using five or six colors with badly overlapping absorption bands, take somewhat longer.

Colorants are selected readily by inspection since the curve shape is constant regardless of concentration (as long as $\theta = KC$). In most

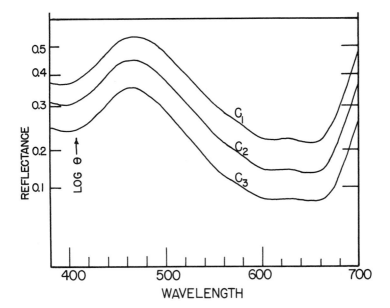

Figure 2.   Log θ = log (1 − R)²/2R. Plot vs. wavelength (nanometers) showing constancy of curve shape at different concentrations C_1, C_3, C_2

instances, colorants for other methods of computation are selected by this method in our laboratory. The curve shape will also be independent of concentration for several other additive functions of the form $\theta = KC^n$.

A number of "improved" forms of the basic θ function can be put into such form; consequently even if the system does not obey the simple Kubelka-Munk equation, equally useful results are obtained. Under these conditions, a correction factor equal to *n* must be applied to the vertical displacement to obtain the true concentration differences.

The details of other methods (*1, 4, 8*) for solving the required equations will not be considered here, but any physical quantity proportional to θ can be used to obtain solution. This may be distance, as in the graphical solutions above, or voltage, as in electrical solutions. Since methods are widely available for accurately controlling and proportioning voltages, the electrical approach is appealing. The electrical analog approach has been developed extensively by Davidson in experiments with analog simultaneous equation solving starting in the early 1950's. These experiments culminated in the commercial production of an ingenious device called COMIC (COlorant MIxture Computer) which permits the solution of 16 simultaneous equations to be observed on an oscilloscope (*8*). While this device is being superseded to some extent by digital computers, some of its features are novel and worthy of mention.

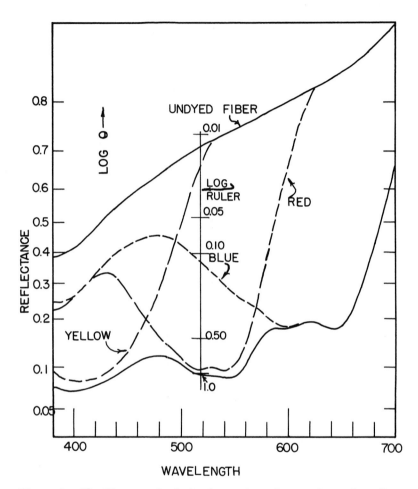

Figure 3. The Pineo method of colorant formulation. Since $\theta = (1 - R)^2/2R$ is an additive function, the combination of yellow, red, and blue necessary to match the standard (solid line) is readily determined. The relative concentrations of each dye are read directly from the transparent logarithmic nomographic scale. In principle, this is the same method used in the D & H COMIC and in digital computer methods where the solution $R_A = R_B$ non-metameric match is desired.

The 16 points displayed are redundant by 11. All that is needed to solve for the concentrations of five colorants are five simultaneous equations with θ_T of V_T at five selected wavelengths. The redundance is necessary to determine whether the correct colorants have been selected by checking the solution at the other 11 points.

The oscilloscope display permits the simple determination of the almost unheard of concept (before high-speed computers)—namely, the best possible solution to 16 simultaneous equations when there is no exact solution. By using auxiliary equipment this "solution" can be made the best possible in a colorimetric sense.

At this point, if all of the assumptions are correct and sufficient precision is maintained throughout, we will have answered the question, "what dyes and how much"? The techniques discussed above and other similar methods permit the entire process (including measurement) to be carried out in 15–20 minutes. At this point we have a trial formulation, not a match on the material at hand.

Until now we have developed a solution only for the special case where $R_a = R_b$ (or only slightly disagrees). If such a solution is impossible because of other requirements such as fastness, price, dyeing process, etc., we must produce a metameric or conditional match. In this case the values of R_b must be adjusted by varying dye concentration and selection so that equality exists for a set of at least six integrals of the form (for X).

$$\int_{400 \text{ nm}}^{700 \text{ nm}} E_c R_a \bar{x} d\,\lambda = \int_{400 \text{ nm}}^{700 \text{ nm}} E_c R_b \bar{x} d\,\lambda$$

Similar equations exist for the tristimulus values Y and Z. If more than one illuminant is of interest, six integrals will be required for each light source.

The reason for the importance of the solution $R_a = R_b$ should be apparent. Since in practice we never really know the value of E or the observer's spectral sensitivity, the only simple general solution possible is where $R_a = R_b$.

Assuming a standard light source and a standard observer, it is possible by various methods to express the difference in tristimulus values $\Delta X, \Delta Y, \Delta Z$ in terms of ΔR (8, 23). The fairly complicated mathematical operation of reducing $\Delta X, \Delta Y, \Delta Z$ to a sufficiently small number by varying ΔR through the functional relation $\theta = f(R) = KC$, can be carried out by modern analog or digital computers by iteration methods. An elegant exposition of the mathematics involved in these methods has been given by Allen (1). Several computer programs have been developed along these lines.

By combining the various approaches outlined above, it is possible, within a few minutes after obtaining the spectral reflectance data on a sample, to obtain a formulation which mathematically satisfies the equations of a simple color match, as outlined in Table I.

Almost any variety of modifications to the basic procedure can be introduced into this system. $\Delta X, \Delta Y, \Delta Z$ can be calculated in a few illuminants, a "metameric index" (17) obtained, and the formulation

altered to obtain the optimum value. A minimum cost formula can also
be calculated. Fastness properties, compatibility with the system, affinity,
etc. can also be built into the combined computer and information retrieval system. The complexity of the calculations for four or more dyes
transcends simple comprehension, but apparently it is within the capability of modern high speed computers.

In favorable cases, the results using any of these methods are straight-
forward. First trials of computed formulations produce matches within
at least three or four color difference units of the standard.

What are the limitations that prevent, at this time, 100% instrumental
match formulation using the simple methods outlined above? Unfortunately, they are fairly numerous and constitute a difficult, if not, insur-
mountable barrier to realizing the goal of color matching solely by reference to instrumental measurements and computation. Some common
causes of difficulty are outlined below.

Failure to obtain a reliable measure of reflectance is one difficulty.
It is caused by lack of correspondence of instrument geometry, with
visual viewing conditions, lack of sensitivity or accuracy of instrument,
and nature of sample with respect to size or texture. Another problem

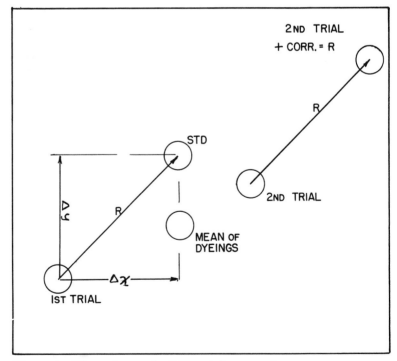

Figure 4.   Effect of reproducibility of dyeing and measurement process
on predicted match

is the failure of (ΔX, ΔY, ΔZ) equal to zero by computation to be equal to zero visually. This is related to the reflectance problem, to metamerism, and to a number of less common problems.

Variation in the dyeing process causes other problems. For a number of reasons, such as concentration errors, fiber variation, and control of the dyebath pH and temperature duplicate dyeings often vary by an amount which exceeds the matching tolerance. This leads to the problems illustrated in Figures 4, 5, 6. When the first trial formulation is dyed, it usually does not match the standard; therefore, a correction must be applied. Since the measured ΔX, ΔY, ΔZ is not the true value owing to the variability of the process, the correction, no matter how mathematically precise, will only produce a match by chance. The probabilities associated with this chance are readily determined once the variances are known.

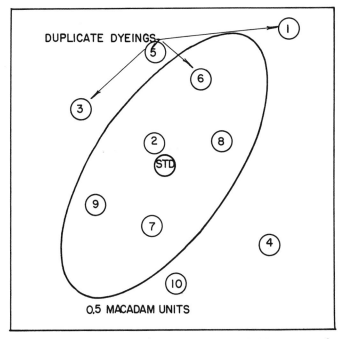

Figure 5. *Variation in dyeings. Dyeings 1–10 were made simultaneously using the standard formula under carefully controlled conditions.*

In addition to the variation of the dyeing process one must consider the variance of the measuring process. Depending on the nature of the sample and the precision of the instrument, this may be smaller or larger than the dyeing variation. On a good instrument with a simple homogeneous sample, this variance can be expected to be about 10% of the

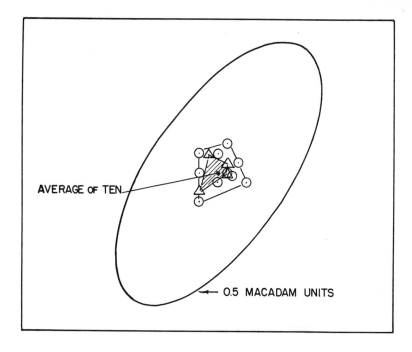

Figure 6.   Variation in repeat measurements on same sample removed and remounted. Comparison of single with means of two measurements.

○ = *Single measurement*
△ = *Mean of two*

variance associated with the dyeing process. Some interesting observations on these matters have been made recently by Marshall and Tough (22). The importance of statistical considerations in all aspects of instrumental color measurement cannot be overemphasized. Figure 6 shows the variation in repeat measurements on a piece of wool flannel. The improvement in variation from the mean, obtained by the simple expedient of comparing the averages of two readings is clearly demonstrated and is close to the theoretical improvement.

In actual practice it is rarely worth making more than four readings on the same sample. The gain in precision is not sufficient to justify the extra time involved. Attempts to produce matches within a smaller tolerance than the sum of the variances is not logical from a statistical viewpoint; however, it is necessary in practice. The color matcher must, by some means, obtain a match that suits the customer no matter how small his tolerance; therefore, he must know that such a match can actually be attained. Experience indicates that a certain formulation may produce a near, but unacceptable, match, but it is not possible to correct the formulation further to attain a better match.

Metamerism is the greatest single cause of disagreement between customer and supplier, regarding the quality of the match. The difficulty a visual color matcher encounters in attempting to produce a metameric match that satisfies the customer (whose spectral sensitivity function is unknown) in several light sources is evident by considering Equation 5.

Figure 7 shows the results of a color matchers' attempt to produce a metameric match as compared with the non-metameric match of the same color. The difficulty with the metameric match is that he is attempting to compromise several illuminants—not just the illuminant C illustrated. In fact, he is not even matching in standard illuminant C, but rather in an artificial daylight lamp (MacBeth), whose spectral energy distribution differs considerably from illuminant C. This is not a factor in the non-metameric case, but it may be critical for the metameric match. Instrumental color matching in the metameric case will produce more consistent results since the instruments experience no such conflict of goals. However, comparison between the instrumental match and a visual match will frequently be poor.

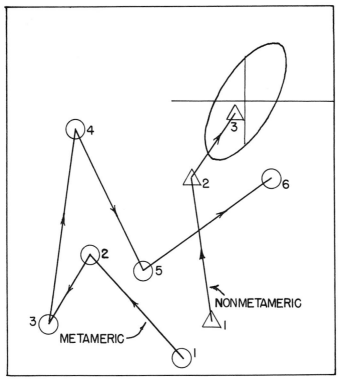

Figure 7.   Comparison of metameric and non-metameric matching with respect to trials and difficulty of attaining match. Ellipse represents "target" match.

The preceding argument is not to be construed as indicating that metamerism should be avoided at all costs; however, it is a major source of rejected material and customer complaints. One should be fully aware of the dangers involved when deliberately producing such matches. It is often noted in the literature that the easiest method to ensure non-metameric matches is to formulate with the same dyes or colorants as in the standard. If more than three dyes are used in the formulation, no insurance against metamerism is provided by this method. It can only be stated that under these conditions, it is possible to produce a non-metameric match. It is also possible to produce a large number of metameric ones. This possibility increases rapidly with the number of colors involved.

Samples which are difficult or impossible to measure are another source of difficulty. Intimate blends containing many colored fibers produce interesting style effects, but matching such a mixture, where the spectral and colorimetric nature of the components is unknown, is extremely difficult. Usually, one has to resort to "microscope matching." Very small samples—portions of prints, mixed yarns, or very small colored areas within a larger sample—are difficult to measure with reliability.

Both instrumental and visual matching of fluorescent materials can be difficult since in this case R is a generally unknown function of E. Thus, it is not possible to measure reflectance under one light source and calculate the results for another, as in the simple color measurement equations where E and R are independent variables. Hence, one cannot expect the precision we have come to expect of non-fluorescent colorimetry. A new variable is introduced, and we have the possibility of a fluorescent metamerism where two samples match under a source which has little effect on R but do not match under a more active source.

Many fabrics contain two, three, or more different fibers. Each of these may be dyed with several different dyes. The ideal circumstance would exist if each set dyed only one fiber or one set dyed them all. Unfortunately, this is rarely the case, and each fiber displays its own relative affinity. This affinity depends on many things and is not independent of the quantity and type of other fibers present. Many practical cases become unbelievably complicated, and again one must resort to the microscope.

Visual effects outside the limits of the simple color measurement equations cause additional difficulties. These problems will not be discussed in detail, but common examples may be found in textile color and design of virtually every color phenomenon or illusion (5, 17). Some of the more common are: simultaneous contrast, spreading effects, area effects, surround and diffuse edge effects. These are all cases where although $(X, Y, Z)_A$ may be equal to $(X, Y, Z)_B$, the samples or areas do not match.

To produce the desired match (or mismatch), it is necessary to produce an ΔX, ΔY, ΔZ different from zero. Unfortunately, the functional relations are not generally available which would permit instrumental formulation of the proper difference to produce the desired color effect.

Present Capabilities. The functional relations and instrumentation are sufficiently developed at present to enable rapid calculation of formulations from basic data where one is given either reflectance or colorimetric data on the material to be matched. Thousands of calculations of this type have been made during the last 20 years, which indicate the validity of the underlying assumptions. The formulations produced by these methods can be expected to produce initial matches within a few color-difference units of the standard in many instances. For the variety of reasons, detailed above, but mainly because of variances inherent in the measurements and the basic data, it is unlikely that much greater precision can be expected. In addition, certain fundamental errors are involved in relating instrumental color measurements to visual results. In the future, one can expect further gains in data acquisition, presentation, and convenience. The complexity of any calculation will provide no deterrent to its usage. The facts and basic data on various colorants will be stored in an easily retrievable state. Thus, the colorist of the future will have available improved instrumentation and computational techniques based on the principles already proved. These will enable him to produce the proper color match more readily and intelligently. It appears, however, that the final arbiter will always be the color sensation produced in the eye and brain of the customer.

In considering the complexity of color-matching, it is not considered likely in the foreseeable future that the entire problem will be handled instrumentally. Rather, the color matcher will be trained in the use of spectrophotometry, colorimetry, and computer methods. These aids will relieve him of much of the routine, sample-matching tasks and enable him to cope more intelligently with the complex. To this extent, it would appear we are on the verge of realizing the vision of the future expressed by Hardy nearly 40 years ago.

Color Control

If color can be measured or quantified, its control becomes a matter of applying the already well-developed methods of statistical quality control. Some sort of a control chart or color map (similar to that shown in Figure 8) is usually employed. A number of ingenious and convenient plotting methods have been devised. Hundreds of thousands of instru-

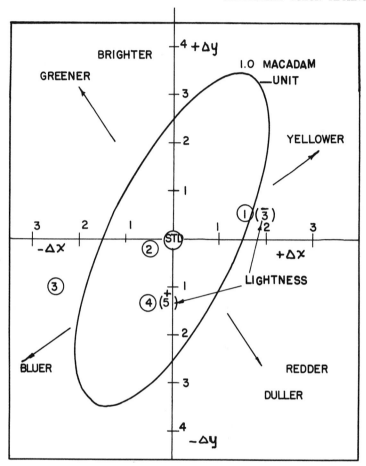

*Figure 8.   Color quality control chart of the four production sam-
ples shown. No. 3 is unacceptable for chromaticity (outside ellipse),
No. 4 for lightness (+5 in parenthesis), and No. 1 is borderline.
The units are Δx, Δy, ΔY × 1000.*

mental color measurements are made each year for this purpose. Their
success provides some confidence in the theory of color measurement.

The ability to record, transmit, and statistically evaluate the control
data is a major advantage of instrumental methods over visual methods.
The limitations on instrumental color control are inherent in the theory
of. color measurements as discussed earlier. A further complication is
difficulty of obtaining meaningful instrumental results on many colored
materials of commercial importance.

The future in this area is well defined. One can expect a steady
advance in the ease of data acquisition, storage, and display. An increased awareness of the power of statistical methods coupled with the
ease of computation will prove rewarding.

Color Tolerances

The problems in this area are not unique to textiles. Fundamentally, the difficulty lies in that there is no universally satisfactory method of specifying, by a single number, the difference in color between two samples. Some equations have been proposed (4) to combine variations in the three dimensions of color to produce a single number which hopefully is proportional to the perceived difference. For small color differences (five units or less) these methods work reasonably well. Our experience indicates that calculations based on MacAdam's data (20) or the Adams-Nickerson Equation (17) are suitable for expressing small color differences. Based on extensive use of MacAdam's data for the last 20 years, we feel that it provides a reliable guide to the relative importance of chromaticity differences. The major problem seems to arise when one attempts to incorporate the lightness term. No simple constant ratio between the lightness difference and the chromaticity seems to produce generally saisfactory results.

The success of the "Grey Scale" method of evaluating color differences would seem to indicate the feasibility of equating a lightness difference to a chromaticity difference. Based on visual experience and examining the data on thousands of samples, it is our feeling that there exists a fundamental problem in that the relation is not constant. Again, for small differences (the smaller the better) this is not a major problem, and consistent results are obtained. Believing that chromaticity differences (ΔC) and lightness differences (ΔL) are fundamentally visually distinct, it is our practice to record these differences separately as well as combined in a "total" color difference (ΔE).

Owing to the fact that the numerical results are not adequately normalized—*i.e.*, the same value of color difference in the yellow and blue regions does not appear visually equal—it is difficult to generalize with respect to tolerances. The following represents an approximate guide based on examining thousands of results in our laboratory:

Close tolerance chromaticity: 0.5–1.0 MacAdam's units lightness 5%

Commercial tolerance chromaticity: 2.0 MacAdam's units lightness 10%

One of the most sensitive areas of color discrimination occurs when the eye is adapted to the color being judged. In practice this occurs when examining large areas of cloth for area shade variations. Such differences produce a condition referred to as "shady," "cloudy," or "streaky" material. Some years ago we demonstrated an excellent correlation between the judgment of inspectors at the mill level and color difference measurements on samples of this type (11). This work was based on the Adams-Nickerson color difference equation, but owing to the small size of the differences, other equations will undoubtedly give satisfactory results.

The tolerances found were (using $f = 100$ in the equation):

ΔE less than 1.0 (blues 0.80) acceptable
ΔE greater than 1.0 less than 2.0 slightly shaded
ΔE greater than 2.0 badly shaded

Another difficulty with color-tolerance specification is that they may not represent a uniform relation to perception differences. Thus, because of preference, knowledge of the end use, etc., certain directions in color space may be tolerated to a greater extent than one would predict, based on perception data. For example, it is almost certain that the green tolerance in the case of meat, borders on the limits of perceptibility, whereas almost any saturation or lightness variation would be tolerated.

When used with care and knowledge, the reduction of colorimetric data to a single number "color difference" can be most useful. However, indiscriminate application of these methods will eventually produce results which are not consistent with visual examination. The ease of evaluating these rather complex equations with modern computers will have a tendency to amplify this problem.

The only important advance to be realized in this area would be improved color-difference equations. Owing to the complexities involved (primarily the weighing between lightness and chromaticity differences) only slow progress, if any, can be expected. In the meantime, considerable utility can be obtained by discrete use of the existing equations, particularly those based on MacAdam's work (21).

Standards

Maintaining standards without recourse to physical samples has always been of interest. If one wishes to specify a homogeneous colored textile by colorimetric data, in order that its shade may be reproduced in the future, great care must be taken in the measurements. We believe it is possible to specify a color on such a basis to within about 3 color difference units. However, this requires careful, well calibrated measurements. Using permanent standards as reference points, the samples should be reproducible within two color difference units. Again, the need for special care and reliable measurement is emphasized if these goals are to be attained.

Color Faults and Their Evaluation

In the daily production of large quantities of colored textiles often consisting of several fibers, each dyed with several dyes, faulty results inevitably arise. The colorist must determine the nature and cause of the problem as rapidly as possible. Spectrophotometry is an indispensable tool in many of these problems. Colorimetry, on the other hand, is of little value since it adds nothing beyond what the eye can readily see. Space is not available to recount the many problems where spectrophotometric analysis, particularly with the aid of the log θ ordinate plot has been the key to a correct and expeditious solution. It suffices to say that we would be handicapped in our daily work without this instrumentation.

In 1900 Paterson stated: "Theoretical knowledge alone cannot make a successful color mixer, but it certainly proves of great value in explaining the true causes of failure and in directing the conditions which lead to success" (*24*). This statement is as true today as it was then. While our sophistication in colorimetry, spectrophotometry, and color science has increased greatly, so have the problems.

The modern colorist must cope with an ever increasing number of new fibers, new dyes, and new finishes. The number of combinations of shade, fiber, and finish becomes large quite rapidly. New demands on chemical stability or fastness places further restrictions on the available solutions. The increasing search by designers for styling and properties with new market appeal leads to evaluation of every conceivable combination. Without the aid of instrumental color measurement, computer color formulation and computer information retrieval, the task facing the colorist or "color mixer" of the future would be formidable if not impossible. To realize the potential of instrumental methods we need more precise and reliable instrumentation, but more important, we need colorists thoroughly trained in the theory and practice of spectrophotometry, color measurement, and color science as applied to the color of textiles.

Literature Cited

(1) Allen, E. R., *Color Eng.* July-Aug. 1966, 15.
(2) Atherton, E., *J. Soc. Dyers Colourists* 1955, 71, 389.
(3) Billmeyer, F. W., Jr., *J. Opt. Soc. Am.* 1965, 707, 55.
(4) Billmeyer, F. W., Jr., Saltzman, M., "Principles of Color Technology," Interscience, New York, 1966.
(5) Burnham, R. W., Hanes, R. M., Bartelson, C. J., "Color: A Guide to Basic Facts and Concepts," Wiley, New York, 1963.
(6) Committee on Colorimetry OSA, "The Science of Color," Thomas Crowell, New York, 1953.
(7) Davidson, H. R., *Am. Dyestuff Reptr.* 1952, 41, 1.
(8) Davidson, H. R., Hemmindinger, H., Landry, J. L. R., *J. Soc. Dyers Colourists 1963*, 79, 577.
(9) Davidson, H. R., Imm, L. W., *J. Opt. Soc. Am.* 1949, 39, 942.
(10) Derby, R. E., Jr., *Am. Dyestuff Reptr.* 1952, 41, 550.
(11) *Ibid.*, 1956, 45, 406.
(12) Derby, R. E., Jr., Fourth Seminar Textile Federation of Canada, 1954.
(13) Evans, R. M., *J. Opt. Soc. Am.* 1964, 54, 1467.
(14) Hardy, A. C., "Handbook of Colorimetry," Technology Press, Cambridge, Mass., 1966.

(15) Hardy, A. C., Perrin, F. H., "The Principles of Optics," McGraw-Hill, New York, 1932.
(16) Judd, D. B., *Color Eng.* **May 1964**, 14.
(17) Judd, D. B., Wyszecki, "Color in Business, Science and Industry," 2nd ed., Wiley, New York, 1963.
(18) Kubelka, P., *J. Opt. Soc. Am.* **1948**, 38, 448, 1067.
(19) Lathrop, A., *J. Opt. Soc. Am.* **1965**, 55, 1097.
(20) MacAdam, D. L., *J. Opt. Soc. Am.* **1943**, 33, 18.
(21) MacAdam, D. L., *Offic. Digest J. Paint Technol.* **1965**, 37, 1487.
(22) Marshall, W. J., Tough, D., *J. Opt. Soc. Am.* **1968**, 84, 108.
(23) Park, R. H., Stearns, E. I., *J. Opt. Soc. Am.* **1944**, 34, 112.
(24) Paterson, D., "The Science of Colour Mixing," Scott, Greenwood, London, 1900.
(25) Pineo, O. W., U. S. Patent **2,218,357** (1940).
(26) Saltzman, M., *Dyestuffs* **1959**, 43, 57-65.
(27) Stearns, E. I., "Analytical Absorption Spectroscopy," M. G. Mellon, Ed., Chap. 7, Wiley, New York, 1950.

RECEIVED June 5, 1969.

Color Formulation and Control in the Vinyl Fabric Industry

FREDERICK T. SIMON

Clemson University, Clemson, S. C.

Vinyl fabrics are basically plasticized poly(vinyl chloride) resin and are found in forms such as film, sheeting, or expanded fabrics. Pigments are used to give the otherwise colorless resin all of the varied effects which can be achieved through mass coloration and/or printing. The texture of the fabric is also modified in many ways by embossing and laminating to other materials. Color control has long been practiced (wherever practical) using the spectrophotometer. Although most of the present instrumentation precludes measurement of metallic, fluorescent, or pearlescent samples, enough is known about the colorimetry of most vinyl fabrics so that the analog and digital computers are used to advantage in color matching and control.

The vinyl fabric industry, as the name implies, produces a variety of fabrics which, like their textile counterparts, find their way into a many decorative and utilitarian applications. These materials are plasticized poly(vinyl chloride) resins that are formed into continuous sheets by calendering, extrusion, or casting and are best known when used as upholstery, wall covering, luggage covering, and shower curtains.

Although this industry is less than 30 years old, there were about 260 million yards of fabric produced in the United States in 1967, and it has an annual rate of growth between 10 and 13% for the past several years. The beginning of vinyls in sheet or fabric form is traceable to the trying days of World War II when substitutes were needed for rubber and oil-coated fabrics which were in short supply. Poly(vinyl chloride) resin had been commercially available as a synthetic resin since 1938, but it was only after World War II that the vinyl fabric industry gained recognition and an impetus of growth brought about by-products that have created their own markets by improvements over the traditional fabrics in functional performance characteristics and durability. All of these applications demand styling to attract the consumer and color as a key element in product appeal.

Vinyls are colored in several ways which relate both to the product form and physical condition of the colorants themselves. The largest volume of vinyl fabrics are made by calendering, the process whereby a thin sheet of plastic is squeezed out continuously between large steel rolls. Arrangements are shown in Figures 1 and 2 of adding colorant to the powdered resin, plasticizer, and stabilizer mixture that eventually

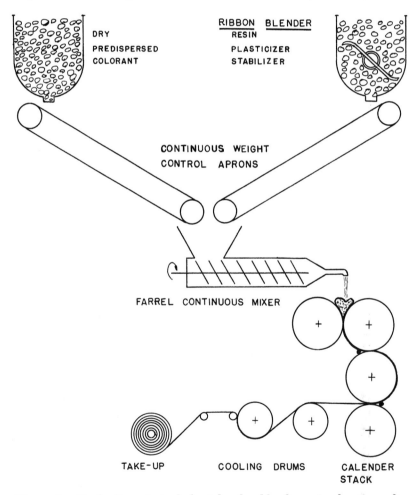

DRY
PREDISPERSED
COLORANT

RIBBON BLENDER
RESIN
PLASTICIZER
STABILIZER

CONTINUOUS WEIGHT
CONTROL APRONS

FARREL CONTINUOUS MIXER

TAKE-UP   COOLING DRUMS   CALENDER
                                        STACK

Figure 1. Production of vinyl sheet by dry blending of color in predispersed form

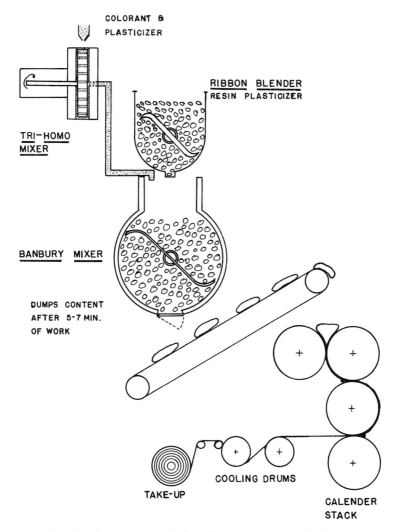

Figure 2.   Production of vinyl sheet by process using Banbury mixer and Tri-Homo mixer for dispersing colorant

ends up as the commercial form of plastic sheet after extrusion. The calendering system itself is not capable of exerting enough work to disperse adequately most pigments into the mass. Therefore, the preparation of the colorant must be done separately and can be accomplished on other equipment in a number of ways. In Figure 1, a dry predispersion is introduced into the calendering stream by weigh-feeding. The predispersion had been made by grinding a pigment with an easily worked vinyl resin to form a pigment concentrate or master batch. This is usually done on some type of attrition mill, and the milled product is reduced further to a fine, granular form. Alternatively, as shown in Figure 2, the pigment powder can be mixed with a portion of the liquid plasticizer and "ground" continuously in a mixer such as the Tri-Homo and metered into the bulk of the resin–plasticizer mixture. There are many variations in the calendering methods, and these are shown as typical installations.

In the past 10 years, considerable development effort has been directed to producing leather-like vinyl fabrics from resin plastisols. This is a different material from the calendered product in that it is made from a poly(vinyl chloride) (PVC) resin which is characterized by its property of absorbing plasticizers easily without the amount of mechanical work necessary with a PVC resin used in calendering.

Vinyls are colored by incorporating pigments into the mass and/or by printing the fabric with pigments dispersed in resins that can bind to its surface. One type of arrangement that is used to produce a vinyl fabric from a plastisol is shown in Figure 3. The resin, plasticizer, sta-

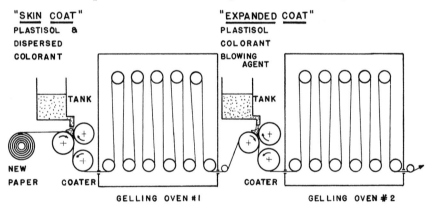

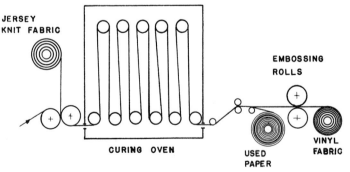

Figure 3.   Manufacture of expanded vinyl fabric by plastisol method

bilizer, and colorants are first mixed together to form a syrup consistency liquid which is cast as a film of desired thickness onto a moving sheet of paper. This film is given a rudimentary form by heating briefly in an oven, causing the plasticizer to dissolve partly in the resin to form a gelatinous film. A second coat can then be cast on the original film, and this usually contains a "blowing agent" which is a substance that will decompose with heat and locally produce small bubbles of gas in the plastic mass. These bubbles expand the second coat to form a spongy mass of lower density. As shown in Figure 3 a knitted cotton fabric can be pressed into the expanded layer, and then the entire sandwich is cured, embossed, and finally stripped from the paper and rolled up. It is possible to vary the fabric construction and physical characteristics over wide limits by modifying the composition and/or the production sequence.

Decoration of vinyl fabrics by rotogravure printing is one of the most common techniques of coloration that has been used in this industry from its beginnings (Figure 4). Printing offers the stylist much flexi-

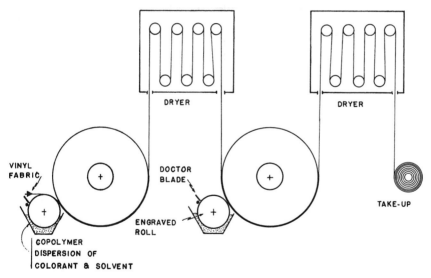

Figure 4.   Printing of vinyl fabrics by rotogravure process

bility in choice of design and color. The inks used to print vinyl fabrics, however, are unique since they must form a bond that is compatible with the fabric surface. Fortunately there are poly(vinyl chloride-vinyl acetate)copolymers which are soluble in organic ketones and can be used for the matrix of pigment dispersion and form a good bond to the vinyl sheet. The printing ink is prepared from a dispersion of the pigment in the copolymer resin plus some harder, acrylic resin, and the entire composition is applied to the vinyl fabric according to the engraved pattern of the print roll. Inasmuch as the "first down" ink must be fairly dry before passing to the next stage of printing, intermediate drying is used to remove the ketone solvent after each color is printed on the fabric.

Although there is great versatility in the vinyl fabric and consequently many applications which impose special requirements on the choice of colorants, the bulk of these materials are colored with inorganic and organic pigments which are generally light fast, and water insoluble. Titanium dioxide is the common opacifying pigment for these coloration systems and is therefore the most important single pigment used by the industry. Other pigments include the inexpensive iron oxides, carbon blacks, and colored lead salts and range to the most expensive fast organic pigments available on the commercial market. Choice of the proper pigment is governed mainly by the application of the vinyl fabric in its final end use. Where a simple colored product might be good enough for a throw-away display item, the severe requirements imposed in automotive upholstery demand the best pigment selection to meet rigid requirements of extreme light fastness.

One of the advantages of the plastic vinyl is its adaptability to coloration by what might be termed "special-effect" pigments. These pigments can be put into the plastic mass of the fabric or into a coating which is applied to the surface of the material after it is formed. Several of the effects that can be obtained are with the fluorescent, pearlescent, and metallic pigments which impart unusual brilliance or directionality to the vinyl and enhance its appearance. The "special effects" are frequently used with the more conventional pigments to effect dramatic color changes which could not be achieved hitherto.

Color measurement is and has been used widely in the vinyl fabric industry, which is one of its heritages from the technologically oriented plastics industry. Almost all of the large vinyl producers use spectrophotometers in both formulation and process color control. The fingerprint identification that the spectrophotometric data give is a valuable clue in selecting the paper colorants which will avoid making a pseudo-color match [conditional or metameric match (1)] that may look different in other illuminants or to various observers. Experience plus a large catalog of spectral data on known colorants serve as the basis of interpretation of the spectrophotometric curve of sample which is to be matched; when this is coupled with knowledge of the fastness characteristics, process behavior, and cost, a group of colorants can be selected which will achieve a spectral match (3).

If one begins with a thorough understanding of the individual colorants, it is then possible to use many of the modern computational tools which help to relieve the color matchers of the more onerous and imprecise trial-and-error procedures of achieving a commercial color match.

Discussions have been given on the use of computers such as the COMIC analog computer and general purpose digital computers for color matching. Many vinyl fabric producers have one or another of these devices in routine operation and generate the type of data that is most suited to their needs. However, it is probably more meaningful to cite a specific example of the use in one plant of the more modern tool for color matching and control. The equipment includes a G. E. recording spectrophotometer, a D and H tristimulus integrator, a D and H COMIC computer, and a digital computer either on a time-share basis or as a conventional "stand-alone" device. With this array of equipment it is possible to put the burden of color matching itself in the hands of the non-technical personnel and therefore utilize the time of the color matcher more effectively. The final formulation for the color match is arrived at with the COMIC analog computer usually in the hands of an experienced color matcher, who has at his disposal the analytical information derived from analysis of the spectral curves of aim and sample. Usually two or three trials are made before a satisfactory match is achieved. For the most part, the question of whether to improve a match or not is guided by calculating the color difference between aim and sample from the colorimetric data obtained with the tris-timulus integrator. The color difference is calculated quickly with a program that is maintained on the digital computer. This is an adaptation of the usual graphical Simon-Goodwin (*2*) method

```
PRESS 'PROGRAM START' BUTTON TO OPERATE


TYPE 1 FOR CCM, 2 FOR CDU, OR 3 FOR BOTH

 2
TYPE COLOR AND NUMBER

 GN1675
TYPE IN AIM, SAMPLE, AND CAM DATA

 2385.2787.5565.2473.2863.5909.100.
HOW MANY SAMPLES DO YOU HAVE

 1
SAMPLE    DELTA  C    DELTA  L    DELTA  A
   1        2.6         1.7         3.1
```

Figure 5. Example of calculation of color difference by a digital computer using Simon-Goodwin (1) constants. The data that are typed into the computer console— or teletypewriter for time share—are enclosed in blocks.

to a general purpose digital method and represents a more rapid and more reliable method. An example of this computation is shown in Figure 5.

When the aim has been matched satisfactorily and approved by the customer, and the material is ready to put into production; a color correction matrix is calculated so that the difference in formulation can be calculated directly from differences in tristimulus data in approved sample and production lot. This matrix is also calculated on the COMIC and serves for the all-important control to assure production of the correct color as successive lots are manufactured. Here again the guide to whether to make correction or not is based on limits expressed in terms of numerical formula which reduces decisions to the common denominator of numerical specification rather than subjective evaluation of competent observers.

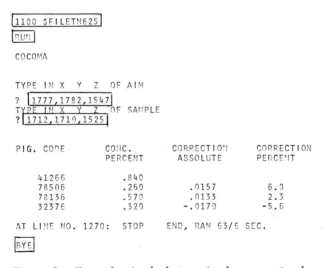

Figure 6.   Example of calculation of color correction by color correction matrix. The data that are typed into the computer console—or teletypewriter for time share—are enclosed in blocks.

The greatest economic incentive for applying scientific color measurement methods comes from the day-to-day control of production. In this environment, time is essential and can be equated directly to costs and potential profits. Figure 6 is a reprint from a computer output where the digital computer is used to store the color correction matrix which is "called" from the computer storage section by the typing in the actual color number, in this case "GN 1675." With the tristimulus data X, Y, and Z for aim and sample also typed in, the computation is performed to tell the operator how much of the various pigments must be added to the sample to match the desired color. This is the technology that makes relatively complicated color control a simple and reliable matter.

Although the manufacture of vinyl fabrics utilizes relatively sophisticated techniques in its production, the end of the loop where color measurements control the process has not been closed except with human intervention. The challenge still remains to complete the servo system and automatically effect color correction with signals read from colorimetric data on continuously produced vinyls; all the elements of a good application seem to be present, but to date no one has succeeded in this effort.

Literature Cited

(1) Billmeyer, Fred W., Jr., Max Saltxman, "Principles of Color Technology," p. 23, Interscience, New York, 1966.
(2) Simon, F. T., Goodwin, W. J., *Am. Dyestuff Reptr.* **1958,** 47, 105.
(3) Wright, W. D., "The Measurement of Colour," p. 139, Adam Hilger, London, 1969.

RECEIVED September 22, 1969.

10

Color Formulation and Control in the Plastics Industry

ROGER P. BEST

Instrumental Colour Systems, Ltd., 42 Kennet Side, Reading, Berkshire, England

Plastics are matched by spectrophotometric data handled by the COMIC analog computer. A tristimulus matrix system from COMIC controls production. Many problems have been solved while others await theoretical and instrumental development. Colorimetry is advancing in Europe as in the United States.

The profitable production of a range of several hundred different colors in thermosetting amino-plastic molding materials, with continual additions being made to this range, demands high efficiency of the color matching and color control systems. Poor initial color matching to a customer's sample can fail to gain new business while poor production color control can lose business by failing to attain the required color difference tolerances. A further monetary loss can be incurred by poor plant utilization resulting from bad color adjusting and from adjusting colors to unnecessarily high tolerance standards.

The industrial colorist in these circumstances ensures that colorant and color adjusting costs are kept as low as is consistent with the quality of the color and the color tolerance required for each particular application. The necessity of using objective means to aid the subjective assessments of the colorist is no longer doubted in the color industry. Even when using traditional methods of color matching, the colorist who applies the precepts of modern colorimetry to his work produces better results in less time.

While the use of precise mathematical models of the behavior of light in turbid media will give good initial color formulating (*1, 8*), other criteria are of greater importance in production color control. The intricacy of the process control calculations must be geared to the means at one's disposal. At plant level the application of a colorimetric control system must be easy and quick to operate and give better results than are obtainable with traditional methods. The color matcher will then use the system as a matter of choice rather than persuasion.

General Methods

Both instrumental colorant formulating and color control at B.I.P. Chemicals is based upon data from the IDL Color-Eye combined abridged spectrophotometer–colorimeter handled by the Davidson and Hemmendinger COMIC analog computer together with a desk calculator in the central color laboratory (Figures 1 and 2). Two production units, one at 100 miles distance, use Color-Eye colorimeters and desk calculators. Information from the central COMIC computer relating to each color to be controlled is sent out to the plants together with a molded plastic working standard and a colorimetric tolerance system.

The initial colorant formulation is done on a spectrophotometric basis through COMIC to ensure minimum metamerism, and corrections are done on a tristimulus basis with the tristimulus difference computing section of COMIC.

This latter facility of COMIC is an obvious method for production color control which can be carried out remotely from the computer with accurate results. To do this for a particular color the TDC (tristimulus difference computer) section of COMIC is used together with the requi-

Figure 1.   Color-Eye colorimeter–spectrophotometer

Figure 2.   COMIC I colorant mixture computer

site three colorant concentration dials and their correction factor dials. A state of balance as shown on the X, Y, and Z difference meters is perturbed by introducing a unit difference in X. The balance is restored by negative or positive additions of the three colorants. These values form the first column of a 3×3 matrix of pre-solved equations of the form first proposed by Stearns (9). The second and third columns are generated similarly for Y and Z.

The resultant matrix of partial derivatives (Equation 1) relating changes in colorant concentrations to unit changes in tristimulus values may be used to correct an off-color batch by multiplying in the tristimulus difference values between batch and standard. In production the colorants are charged to a batch at about 80% of their nominal full value, leaving the Color-Eye and matrix system to give a color adjustment to bring the batch on color. This method is very tolerant of slight deviations in the hue and strength of colorants and copes with large deviations in the color of the base material. Colorant additions given by this means reduce the tristimulus differences almost to zero, thus giving a visual match.

$$\frac{\delta\,c_1}{\delta\,X} \times \Delta\,X + \frac{\delta\,c_1}{\delta\,Y} \times \Delta\,Y + \frac{\delta\,c_1}{\delta\,Z} \times \Delta\,Z = \Delta\,c_1$$

$$\frac{\delta\,c_2}{\delta\,X} \times \Delta\,X + \frac{\delta\,c_2}{\delta\,Y} \times \Delta\,Y + \frac{\delta\,c_2}{\delta\,Z} \times \Delta\,Z = \Delta\,c_2$$

$$\frac{\delta\,c_3}{\delta\,X} \times \Delta\,X + \frac{\delta\,c_3}{\delta\,Y} \times \Delta\,Y + \frac{\delta\,c_3}{\delta\,Z} \times \Delta\,Z = \Delta\,c_3 \qquad (1)$$

where c_1, c_2, c_3 relate to the three colorants in the mixture.

The use of this matrix of "tinting factors" assumes linearity between small measured differences in tristimulus values between standard and batch and the effect of additions of colorants. While this is not strictly true, the lack of linearity is insignificant over small movements in color space.

Having achieved good results with an instrumental control system the production color matcher may then decide that he can improve these results with a visual adjustment. This is a natural human reaction to an instrumental system and can be avoided only by providing a colorimetric tolerance control system. From the many so-called uniform color scales available (7), few are easily applicable unless a programmable desk calculator or a computer is always available.

Some Problems and their Solutions

The plastics industry shares problems of color measurement and deficiencies in the CIE system with the paint and textile industries. It also has its own particular problems which, while few, bar progress until they are solved.

The simple K/S ratio function of Kubelka and Munk although apparently fairly linear with colorant concentration, does not work well for plastics. A correction for reflectance errors (10) improves matters, but the empirical corrections to K/S proposed by Davidson and Hemmendinger (4) give the best results with COMIC. The use of $(K/S)^{1.25}$ enables first predictions to be made that are well balanced—*i.e.*, are of almost the required hue. A subsequent tristimulus difference correction easily corrects chroma (saturation) and value (lightness).

A problem which seems to be found only in plastics is the matching and control of translucent media. Theoretically one may say that with a single function of reflectance the instrumental matching of transparent media is easy, that of opaque media is difficult, and that of translucent media is impossible. For the K/S ratio to be additive and linear with colorant concentration, constant scatter is assumed. This is lost as soon as the white pigment is low or zero. The scatter will then change as the concentrations of colorants change, thus introducing apparent chaos. This is not improved by the impossibility of determining the reflectivity of the sample. (The measured reflectance of sample is applicable only in the Kubelka-Munk equation $(1-R)^2/2R$ if the sample is of a hiding thickness—*i.e.*, if it is equal to the reflectivity.) Edge-loss errors when measuring a translucent sample can be as high as 25% (2), thus complicating matters further.

The first step in bringing order into this situation is to ensure that the basic colorant information being given to the computer is reliable. It was found that with moldings 2 mm thick and 5 inches square a concentration of 0.2% titanium dioxide was the optimum loading for minimum edge loss. Atkins and Billmeyer (2) found that the optimum loading for 1 mm thickness is 0.1% and for 4 mm is 0.4% of titanium dioxide.

All colorant information programmed into the computer is based on this loading of 0.2% titanium dioxide on the plastic base on samples 2 mm thick and 5 inches square. To reduce further the consequences of edge loss, a series of trials was made to determine the best material for backing the translucent samples in the measuring port. While black is the correct color, neutral greys gave better results as they increased in reflectance. The best, with all degrees of translucency, proved to be a glossy white vitrolite tile. This is used for all samples which transmit light and are of 2 mm thickness. The production control of translucent colors is much easier than it apparently should be, as long as care is taken to ensure that the titanium dioxide content in the batch is identical to that of the standard and of the same type as that on which the control system is based. A change in the type of titanium dioxide will render the system useless.

An associated problem peculiar to plastics is the strange effect given by increasing the white pigment and the colored pigments by the same factor. The resulting plastic will be much deeper in color. This arises from the small amounts of white commonly used. If a series of molded samples are prepared with a constant amount of colored pigment, say 0.1% ultramarine blue, but with varying amounts of titanium dioxide ranging from zero to say 7.0%, then at the wavelength of maximum absorption—*i.e.*, lowest reflectance—the effect on the $(K/S)^{1.25}$ value can be tabulated. The unit concentration of white for computer information being set at 0.2%, the $(K/S)^{1.25}$ of this is divided into the $(K/S)^{1.25}$ values of all the other white loadings. These ratios times 100 plotted against the TiO_2 content on a log-log scale will give a straight line (Figure 3). For matching plastics of any particular white content the corresponding ratio $\times$ 100 value, gives the correction factor to be set on the colorant correction factor dials of COMIC. This correction method, besides allowing for the nonlinear covering power of the white pigment, also seems to correct the change in scatter caused by the variations in white pigment. It is surprisingly successful.

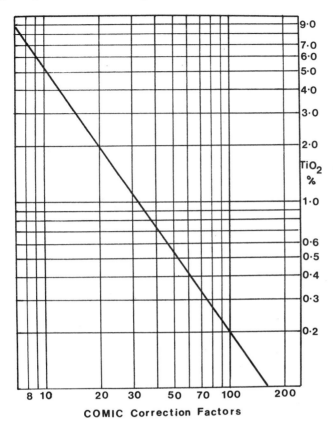

Figure 3. Method of utilizing colorant information based on a particular white loading for any other white content

Another problem particularly acute in the coloration of plastics is the change of chroma and hue experienced with pigment development as it is dispersed in the medium. This change appears to be related to pigment particle size, organic pigments being worse than inorganic pigments. The only solution is precise correlation between laboratory and production scale units. There is no short cut, particularly with processes that use ball mills to incorporate pigments since color development is continuous until primary particle size is achieved and particle distribution is uniform. Since the development is not linear with time, the time factor is of obvious importance if the color is to be "caught as it runs," and it is advantageous to work on a fairly flat part of the development curve if at all possible.

A problem not exclusive to plastics but shared by all who venture into this field is the difficulty of matching and controlling dark colors.

For prediction of dark colors the determination of K (absorption) and S (scatter) is required since the K/S ratio calculated from $(1-R)^2/2R$ is not sufficiently linear. Batch control with tristimulus difference values can be very good if a matrix generated from separate K and S data is used. Another difficulty in dark color control is measurement. The exclusion of the gloss or specular component of the reflected light is obtained in most measuring instruments that have integrating spheres by a small black insert or cap. If the surface being measured has any irregularities, some of the specular component of the reflected light escapes this black insert and is included with the diffuse component. The amount that is included will change as the sample changes position in the measuring port. With light colors where the diffuse component is high, the escaping specular component is unimportant, but with dark colors of fairly high gloss and low diffuse component the errors introduced are serious. Attempts have been made to reduce these errors by measuring an area of the sample made matt by vapor blasting the mold, also by including the whole of the specular component by replacing the black insert with a white one.

This latter method of including the specular component combined with the substitution method of measurement, as recommended by the manufacturers of the Color-Eye colorimeter for maximum precision, gives better repetition of measurement on dark colors than can be obtained any other way.

Some idea of the inherent disadvantage under which instruments work as compared with the eye on colors reflecting less than 3% of the incident light can be seen in Figure 4. This comparison of the objective and subjective uniform neutral grey scales obtained by plotting the visually equal steps of Munsell values against the lightness (Y) of this scale as measured with the General Electric recording spectrophotometer with the Davidson and Hemmendinger tristimulus integrator (5), shows that 1/4 of the visual scale is compressed into 1/20 of the instrumental scale.

Careless color formulating, while rendering visual matching difficult, destroys instrumental control. The sort of thing to be avoided is a grey consisting of a black, white, and an orange and a red toning pigment. The color gamut triangle of such a combination is very narrow and cannot cope with the variations of production. A grey for precise instrumental control, as for easy visual matching, requires besides black and white colorants, three primaries—preferably blue, yellow, and orange/red. On all colors good trichromatic control which at the same time is not too delicately balanced will ensure instrumental tristimulus control.

Certain bright colors will not tolerate more than two colorants. These can be controlled visually with fair success, but, surprisingly, even better

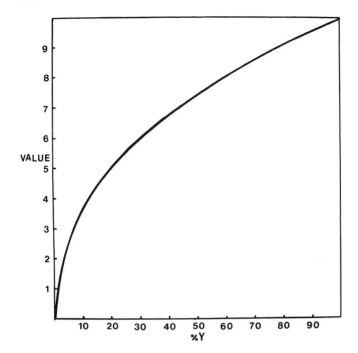

Figure 4. Visual vs. *instrumental lightness comparison of neutral grey scale*

results are obtained by colorimetry. To generate a matrix on COMIC, a third colorant is required to balance the tristimulus difference meters. Black acts perfectly as a mathematical operator, the consequent third row of the 3 × 3 matrix being discarded. It generally sums to zero anyway.

A problem that can upset any colorimetric control system is the different utilization factors of colorants when they are added to the base medium and when they are added to an off-color batch. The difference is illustrated well by the difference in colorant correction factors obtained from COMIC in these different circumstances. It is so important that the correction factors to be used when utilizing COMIC to adjust a batch of material or generate a control matrix should always be determined by making a reduction of about 20% in the color to be controlled, replacing the missing colorants and balancing the consequent difference in tristimulus values and the difference in colorants with the correction factor dials. This is a simple and quick laboratory operation which pays dividends in production control, providing precise correlation exists between small and large scale color mixing or blending.

To normalize a matrix generated on COMIC by these means each column relating to a particular tristimulus difference value must be divided by the value used. The column will then relate to a unit change in tristimulus value. The unit matrix may then be used directly, or its elements may be multiplied by some factor which relates to the charge weight of the batch of material being corrected, thus giving a direct read-out in weights to be added to the batch.

A useful check on the figures in the matrix, when using this method, is to sum the rows before normalization. These sums should be almost identical to the actual colorant differences between the reduced and the full shade. The small differences obtained through the analog working of the computer are found to be far below visual perception levels. Any gross error indicates that a mistake has been made in generating the matrix.

Possibly the most serious problem concerns the lack of linearity between the addition of colorants and the consequent changes in tristimulus values. While this lack of linearity is insignificant over small movements in color space, it is significant in production control when a batch is way off color.

When using the TDC of COMIC I to correct a color or when using a matrix of "tinting factors" generated either by COMIC, or as the by-product of a digital program, or even a matrix obtained by the hand inversion of a matrix obtained experimentally describing changes in tristimulus values given by changes in colorants, the result is always the same. If the color is close to the standard, the resultant match is unacceptable. If the color is far away, the result of the correction will be unacceptable. With a stronger color the result will be an undershoot in the degree of colorant change, still giving a darker color. In production control however a weaker color is always the aim so that colorant additions may be made to bring the batch up to the full and correct shade without adding extra white pigment. Such an addition is objectionable for several reasons, one being the differing opacities which would result from this technique. It is unfortunate therefore that a weaker color, far from the standard, when corrected, always overshoots, thus ruining the batch. If the color movement is broken down into steps, only a fraction of the adjustment is added at a time, and the results are plotted in CIE space, they follow a smooth path with some colors passing near the target and with others passing wide. An obvious cure is to halt the series of steps in the region where they are nearest the target zone. Since this varies from color to color and time prohibits small steps, a simple expedient is to cut the first colorant addition to a batch that is way off target by half. In the production of many thousands of batches of material this has never failed and never caused an overshoot. Experience has shown that this is a safe level. Even a rise to 60% of the indicated colorant addition would have caused some batches to be rejected.

After the first 50% addition has been made, the color will, except on a few occasions with dark colors, be near enough to the target to complete the matching to within very close tolerances in one full matrix adjustment. Figure 5 shows an initial matching where adjustments to the first prediction, which was poor because of metamerism, were made normally (A) and by the two-stage method (B). The plot in CIE space shows that the full first correction on this mauve color caused a bluer and deeper overshoot. The second correction was pinker and lighter, and the third approached a close visual match of 1 MacAdam unit. In B the 50% correction fell short of the target, being pinker and lighter but the second, full correction gave the same result as achieved in A but with less effort and yielded an identical colorant formulation.

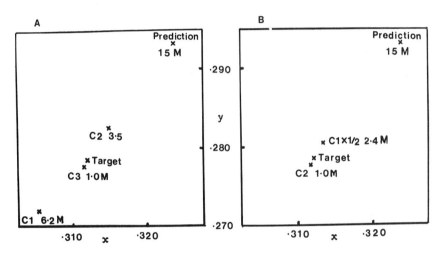

Figure 5.   Initial matching (Munsell 7P 6.5/5). Initial match prediction, 15 MacAdam units. With normal iteration, three corrections are required for 1 MacAdam unit match (A). With first correction halved, only two are required (B).

Figure 6 shows the result of a two-stage correction to a dark khaki brown. A small sample was taken from the batch so that the result of a full first correction rather than a 50% one could be shown. This full correction resulted in a serious overshoot, which being darker would have ruined the batch of material had it been applied.

Since it is not always necessary to use this two-stage approach to the target color, limiting values for its application must be indicated in the control system. Occasionally, on dark colors, these limiting values are not achieved after the first color adjustment, and a further half adjustment is required before the final full matrix adjustment is applied. Three color adjustments may seem tedious, but this is the type of color which

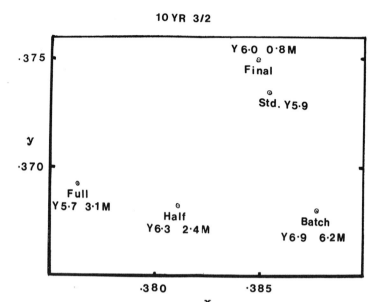

Figure 6. *Production control. Full matrix adjustment overcorrects. Half-step followed by full step gives good match (two-stage method).*

often requires up to seven visually assessed adjustments, giving a final color which is only barely satisfactory.

Indicating precise limiting values for using this two-stage system is both difficult and perhaps not entirely necessary. Conversion of the tristimulus difference values to a uniform chromaticity–luminosity scale is desirable to set the limits, but a simple single-value top limit for a ratio difference in X, Y, and Z suffices. This changes with different colors from a reflectance of about 108% on some light colors to 120% or higher on dark colors.

The problem of setting instrumental color tolerance limits is difficult because of the nonlinear relationship between CIE and visual color space and because commercial tolerance limits are not always simple expansions of the just noticeable difference ellipsoids of CIE color space (7). A further problem for plants without some means of quickly computing uniform chromaticity–luminosity scale units such as is provided by the Davidson and Hemmendinger color difference computer (CODIC) is the time required for hand calculation. Graphical methods are essential for speed in these circumstances.

A safe method is shown in Figure 7 where the differences in chromaticity coordinates, Δx and Δy are plotted against ΔY. The ellipses are set up from information on many previously acceptable batches. However the calculation of Δx and Δy can be too time consuming. A simplified plot of ΔX ratio *vs.* ΔY ratio and ΔZ ratio *vs.* ΔY ratio (Figure 8) based upon previously accepted batches is quick to use but occasionally breaks down.

If, as with instrumental control, close tolerances are easily obtained, then MacAdam units as calculated with the Columbus Coated Fabrics Speed Charts (6) are very effective. These use only Y ratio–X ratio and Y ratio–Z ratio readings. Versions of these enlarged by 2 to aid the plotting of small distances in color space are proving successful despite the fact that a difference of say 2 MacAdam units in one direction in color error appears more or less visually acceptable than a similar difference in another direction. With the precision of color matching given by colorimetric control of colorant additions, a tolerance set in the most noticeably different direction of color error can be met easily so that this objection is not serious.

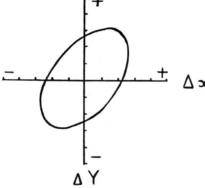

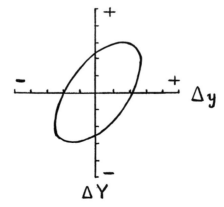

Figure 7. Color tolerance ellipses based on chromaticity coordinate and luminosity data

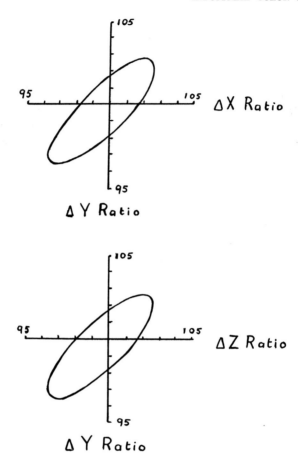

Figure 8.   *Color tolerance ellipses based on tri-*
stimulus ratio differences

The tolerance in MacAdam units must be set for each color on a range. Once experience is gained in a particular sector of color space the setting of meaningful tolerances becomes simple and quick, much less wasteful of laboratory time than drawing ellipses based upon previous batches. With new additions to the color range the advantage of this method is obvious.

Results

A typical run on a bright pink plastic (Munsell 7.5RP 8/6) shows the sort of color variation which is often encountered from batch to batch and the efficacy of the control system.

Batch	Color Difference, (MacAdam units)		Correction Stages Required
	Initial	Final	
1	7.3	0.6	1
2	11.0	1.3	2
3	4.2	0.9	1
4	7.0	0.5	1
5	7.0	2.1	1
6	4.0	1.8	1
7	4.1	1.3	1
8	13.8	1.3	2
9	13.8	2.3	2

The tenth batch of initial color difference of 11.6 MacAdam units which indicated that the two-stage approach was required was deliberately charged with the full pigment instead of 50%. The results was an overshoot to 3.7 MacAdam units. It was rejected by the tolerance system and by visual inspection.

Future Research and Development

To eliminate some current problems, the CIE system must be modified and further instrument development is necessary. With neutral colors, including creams, one can find even with little metamerism that

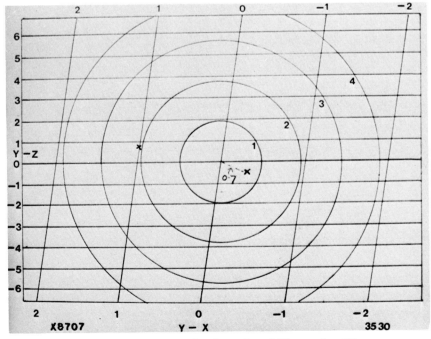

Figure 9. Columbus Coated Fabrics Speed Chart color difference

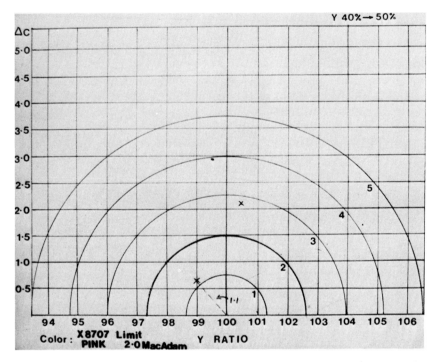

Figure 10.   Columbus Coated Fabrics Speed Chart. Color difference corrected for luminosity.

a match in terms of tristimulus values is not visually acceptable. The more general adoption of the D6500 illuminant and 10° field observer data would probably help to bring colorimetry more closely into line with what we see, but it is unlikely that source "C" and 2° field observer data are the real cause of this trouble. The CIE $\bar{z}$ function as it stands could easily be the reason since it is always a difference in yellowness that causes this anomaly. The inability of the $\bar{z}$ function to separate the easily visible yellowness difference between anatase and rutile forms of titanium dioxide is discussed by Blakey (3). There seems to be a real need for functions which relate more closely to the true sensitivities of the retinal cones.

The measuring instruments themselves have one major defect in their application to plastics. This is the small size of the sample viewing area. A visual assessment taken over a large area of 25 square inches automatically integrates the small color variations over the surface of a sample. When these differences exist, as they do frequently on darker colors, the general effect is what should be measured. This would require an instrument with a large viewing port such as that on the I.D.L. large sphere Color-Eye but with the same precision as the small sphere model.

To control dark colors to a visually acceptable degree, even greater instrument sensitivity will be required, together with separate K and S summation.

While remarkable results can be and are being achieved with colorimetry as it is practiced today, the rewards of these developments could give full instrumental control over the whole color gamut.

Installations of the Future

For small runs of colored plastics materials the batch system will always have some advantages particularly in cleaning down time, but large runs of popular colors will be more economical on continuous processes. For these, fully automatic color control will be essential, otherwise the advantages of the process will be lost in poor plant utilization.

The specialized digital computing equipment of the future is already available in the form of COMIC II. Our experience, even with the analog COMIC I, has been that this is the strongest link in the colorimetric theory, measurement, and computing chain.

With COMIC II, data may be fed automatically from the digital readout of a measuring instrument. Ideally this would be in spectrophotometric reflectance ratio form, leaving the computer to calculate the colorant changes, if any, required for a visual match to preset tolerances. The meters measuring the flow of material to be colored and the colorants would be linked to the computer. Possibly the most difficult step before such an arrangement becomes practicable is the automatic and rapid preparation of a sample in a suitable form for measurement.

Colorimetry in Europe

Since European color measuring and computing equipment is rarely seen in the United States, the general position in Europe may be of some interest. The use of American equipment is widespread, but there are a few European firms now producing measuring and computing equipment. The application of colorimetry as it is known to the author is set out under industrial headings.

Colorant Producers

Colorimetry is used by titanium dioxide manufacturers to determine the scatter coefficient and hiding power of their products, this being an essential part of their quality control systems.

The larger producers of dyes and pigments use spectrophotometry to blend batches, thus ensuring that the final batches have spectral characteristics as nearly identical as possible.

Textiles

The application of colorimetry to color matching appears to be concentrated largely on initial formulation where both COMIC I and digital computer systems are used. In the large textile companies the volume of work is so high that it almost precludes the possibility of returning a color-matching job to the computer for a correction to the initial prediction. This is generally left to the laboratory colorist to do visually. Final corrections to textile colors are further complicated by the difficulty of obtaining precise and meaningful measurements of textured surfaces. The Instrumental Match Prediction service of I.C.I. for users of their dyes provides both an initial dye recipe and a color correction matrix.

Paints

A few firms are successfully controlling production of light-to-medium depth colors with either narrow waveband spectral data or with tristimulus data. COMIC and digital computers are used for initial match prediction while color tolerance systems of various types are used to set drift limits.

Plastics

The difficulty of preparing samples with the good repeatability so necessary for instrumental control is one difficulty with thermoplastics, another being the problem of the variations experienced with each individual color blending machine or extruder. However work is progressing on these problems, and colorimetric tolerance control systems are already in operation, using mainly differential colorimeters.

The realative ease with which good samples can be prepared in thermosetting materials has aided the application of colorimetric control to this section of the industry.

Valiant efforts are being made in the industry to control the production of vinyl coated fabrics by colorimetry, but difficulty is being encountered with textured surfaces and the dark colors that are used for automobile upholstery. No doubt digital computers combined with sensitive measuring instruments with large viewing ports will eventually solve these problems.

Paper, Inks, and Cosmetics

Only the paper industry seems to have had much success with colorimetry, and steady progress is reported. Unfortunately the darker colors which give trouble to visual color matchers are those in which the most of the interest lies and it is these which cannot yet be measured with the necessary precision.

Conclusion

It is unfortunate that the lighter colors which are most easily controlled by instruments are also those for which the visual color matcher finds adjustment easy. The general reaction of the traditional color matcher is: why bother with all this complicated and expensive equipment? However the ultimate objective of colorimetry is the rapid and precise control of all colors, including those on which the visual color matcher wastes considerable time, generally ending up with poor color drift tolerances. While colorimetry is now an indispensable tool in the color matching laboratory, its progress in production color control is somewhat slower owing to the difficulties of applying laboratory techniques on a large scale and yet making them simple and rapid to apply while ensuring practically 100% success. Considerable progress has now been made with this difficult task, and as in all fields of human endeavor progress accelerates as knowledge accumulates.

Literature Cited

(1) Atkins, J. T., Billmeyer, F. W., Jr., *Color Eng.* **1968**, 6 (3), 40–47, 56.
(2) Atkins, J. T., Billmeyer, F. W., Jr., *Mater. Res. Std.* **Nov. 1966**, 6, 11.
(3) Blakey, R. R., *J. Soc. Dyers. Colourists* **1968**, 84, 120.
(4) Davidson, H. R., Hemmendinger, H., *Color Eng.* **1966**, 4, 3.
(5) Davidson, H. R., Hemmendinger, H., "Data for Use with Munsell Color Book," Davidson & Hemmendinger, 1962.
(6) Foster, R. L., *Color Eng.* **1966**, 4 (1).
(7) MacKinney, G., Little, A. C., "Color of Foods," Avi Publishing Co., Westport, Conn.
(8) Orchard, S. E., *J. Oil Color Chem. Assoc.* **1968**, 51, 44.
(9) Park, R. H., Stearns, E. I., *J. Opt. Soc. Am.* **1944**, 34, 112.
(10) Saunderson, J. L., *J. Opt. Soc. Am.* **1942**, 32, 727.

RECEIVED June 6, 1969.

11

Color Formulation and Control in the Paint Industry

SAM J. HUEY

Color and Standards Laboratory, The Sherwin-Williams Co.,
101 Prospect Ave., N.W., Cleveland, Ohio 44101

The trial and error method of selecting the proper pigments for paint color formulation is being augmented by the use of color measuring instruments and computers utilizing the Kubelka-Munk equation. This is also true of production color matching in the factory. To take full advantage of these new techniques, good standards must be available. To have standards that are satisfactory for instrument measurement and long time color stability, certain precautions must be followed. Numerical tolerances can be established for color control, but their limitations must be considered. Buyers of industrial finishes are not only concerned with the magnitude of the color difference but the direction the color is from the standard. This requires alterations to the present color difference equations.

Probably no other industry has such a wide choice of colorants to meet its customers' requirements as the paint industry. Some paint producers have an active list of over 300 colored pigments, and inventories of more than 200 are not uncommon. Producers of even relatively limited lines of paints use more than 100 different pigments, yet it is generally agreed that most of today's colors could be made with as few as 20 pigments. The "Munsell Book of Colors" underscores this point. This gamut of the visible spectrum consists of approximately 1600 colors and was made with only 20 pigments. One pigment manufacturer claims that most colors could be matched with the 16 pigments he recommends.

Why, then, do paint manufacturers have so many different colored pigments? Simply because many factors other than color must be considered in selecting a paint colorant. Alkali resistance, light fastness, heat stability, ease of dispersion—all of these characteristics and others can vary considerably for pigments of approximately the same hue. Hence, a wide choice of colored pigments is necessary to provide the formulator with the building blocks needed to construct a product that meets the specifications.

Pigment Selection in Color Formulation

Paint formulators today can arrive at the proper choice of pigments to match a given color by two routes. One is the time-tested method of experience; the other is by using color measuring instruments and computers. The second approach is gradually replacing the first.

Regardless of which method he will follow, the formulator always starts with a sample of the color he wishes to reproduce. This may be a standard panel or color chip, a coated manufactured item, a piece of fabric, or anything else that will show him the color required. Knowing the color, the formulator must consider what other qualities the paint should have. What durability characteristics are needed? What application method will be used? Will the paint be air dried or baked? Is resistance to specific chemicals required? What are the cost limitations? The answers to all such questions will determine the multitude of ingredients used to make up the complex paint film. They will also narrow considerably the large list of pigments available for the formulation.

Color Formulation through Experience

An experienced formulator usually starts with a reasonably good idea of those pigments he needs to match the color and those pigments that will enable him to meet the other requirements of the finished product. He also knows that unless he relies on sophisticated instrumentation, he will probably have to undergo considerable trial and error before he finds the exact combination of pigments for his purpose. When a decision has been reached concerning the pigments and other ingredients, a small laboratory batch—perhaps one gallon—will be made. The equipment used must be selected carefully so that the results will be reproducible for a large production batch (50–6000 gallons). Frequently, many laboratory batches must be made before the right combination of pigments is established. The task becomes more difficult when a spectral match is required.

Just as frequently, the laboratory batch may have the correct pigments but not the correct amount. It will then have to be shaded with more of the same colors originally used until the desired color is obtained. In some cases, the color may have to be adjusted by adding other colors. Such additions can affect other characteristics required in the paint. When the laboratory batch is satisfactory for color and all other characteristics, a production-batch formula is written.

With some reservations, one could say the foregoing procedure is a trial and error method and not very scientific. However, this has been the standard practice in the paint industry and is still being used to a great extent. While it is fairly simple, it is extremely time consuming. Hence, more efficient methods are required.

Color Formulation by Spectrophotometry

One step toward more efficient color formulation was taken some years ago when the role of the spectrophotometer was explored. Increased experience with this instrument led to its expanded use (*4*). However, despite the more scientific procedures it fosters, this type of instrumentation by itself does not eliminate reliance on trial and error. For example, certain inherent characteristics of the spectrophotometric curves of pigments are not lost in the curves of combinations of various pigments. Therefore, by comparing curves of known pigments (letdown in white) with the curves of the pigments in the standard, it is possible to identify the pigments in the standard with a fair degree of accuracy. However, this is only part of the problem. Once the pigments are identified, the formulator still must rely on his experience in determining the quantity of each pigment needed. Often he is wrong, and the additions and adjustments must be made by trial and error.

Even in the early stages of formulation by spectrophotometry, there was another way to determine quantitative requirements—*i.e.*, by using the Kubelka-Munk equations. There were isolated cases where paint chemists were using this method, making the complicated calculations by longhand or with desk calculators. However, the time required for this was an extremely limiting factor. As a result, efforts along this line were confined to handling only a token amount of the total color matching.

Color Formulation by Colorimetry and Computers

In 1957 Davidson and Hemmendinger introduced their analog computer capable of solving the Kubelka-Munk equations. This triggered a whole new concept of quantitative color matching in the paint industry. For the first time both the pigments and the quantity needed to match a batch of paint could be determined with sufficient speed to make the procedure practical in development and production color matching. Many paint companies are still successfully using the analog computers produced by Davidson and Hemmendinger.

Development of even faster digital computers suggested that these too could be used for color matching. However, initially it was generally felt that such computers could not be used exclusively for color matching because of their high cost. If they were installed for other purposes and computer time became available, they were used to solve color problems. Fortunately, this phase was short lived. It was soon obvious that the time saving, coupled with better formulas and color control, amply justified the use of digital computers for color and its related problems.

The shift to digital computers was not without confusion and centered chiefly on questions of what program and computer should be used. Eventually, it became apparent that such matters were secondary. The real problem was—and still is—how to use most effectively the knowledge and equipment available. As Max Saltzman, co-author of "Principles of Color Technology," has pointed out, the type of computer is not too important at this state of the art. More important is the need for good data. This requires good standards, accurate instruments, and good techniques.

Checking New Shipments of Colored Pigments

For computer formulation to be successful, uniform color pigments are necessary. Once a specification has been set up, newly received pigments should not vary by more than the tolerance permitted. Thanks to the advent of new methods of preparing samples for color evaluation, color specifications and tolerances can now be established more readily than heretofore.

These new methods, several of them under evaluation by ASTM, include the example: Sub 26, Group 21, "Pigment Color by Miniature Sand Mill." Their advantage over the time-tested Hoover-Mueller method is that they more easily provide samples large enough to prepare adequate panels (8). Preparation of information for computer comparison of the standard and the newly received pigment is relatively simple. After the new pigment is dispersed in TiO_2 and a suitable vehicle, a drawdown of the dispersed material is made, and the tristimulus values X, Y, Z are obtained from a dried sample. The reflectance of the sample at the wavelength of maximum absorption is also determined. The same data are required in regard to the standard.

Figure 1, a facsimile of a printout from the General Electric Time Share computer, illustrates the computer output. The information appears in an established sequence: (1) comparison of the tinting strength of the sample with the standard at the wavelength of maximum absorption; (2) the hue and saturation difference (ΔC); (3) the total color difference (ΔE) in MacAdam units; (4) the ratio of the tristimulus values of the sample compared with the standard—if the sample and standard matched perfectly this would read 100,100,100; (5) the hue of the standard; (6) direction of variation of the sample from the stand-

```
XYZ ØF STD?
?  80.01,85.08,52.29
XYZ ØF SAMPLE?
?  79.56,84.88,50.21
R ØF STANDARD, R ØF SAMPLE AND WAVELENGTH?
?  41.4,39.3,440

SAMPLE IS 13.03 % STRØNG @ 440

DELTA C=          2.41
DELTA E=          2.42

RATIØS= 99.4   99.8   96

STD HUE IS YELLØW

SAMPLE IS GREENER            DELTA H= 2.35   75.8 %
SAMPLE IS MØRE SATURATED     DELTA S= 0.52   16.9 %
SAMPLE IS DARKER             DELTA L= 0.23   7.3 %

STANDARD DØMINANT WAVELENGTH= 573.87 NM
PERCENT PURITY= 35.77 %

SAMPLE DØMINANT WAVELENGTH= 573.75 NM
PERCENT PURITY= 37.55 %
```

Figure 1. Complete color difference description of an incoming shipment of pigment as compared with the standard

ard in terms of the three dimensions of color and the percentage of variation of each attribute in the total color difference; (7) the dominant wavelength and percent purity of the standard; (8) the dominant wavelength and percent purity of the sample (6). The last two items provide a check on the statement regarding hue and saturation.

Such complete information provides a detailed statement of how the sample differs from the standard. If there is a case for rejection, it is spelled out in the kind of precise terms that make communication between purchaser and supplier much more meaningful than the usual "the sample is off in color."

Preparation of a Pigment Library

Another necessary preliminary step toward successful computer formulation is the development of a pigment library. This consists essentially of data derived from a series of spectrophotometric curves on each of the pigments normally available to the formulator. It is from these data that the computer selects pigments needed to match a given color. The pigments are dispersed in a suitable vehicle. Then letdowns are made with a dispersed white in concentrations of colored pigment to the TiO_2 in the white as follows: .04%, .01%, 1.0%, 4.0%, 10.0%, 30%, 70%, and 100% or what is called the masstone.

Spectrophotometric curves are run on the letdowns at each concentration, and the reflectance at 16 equidistant points across the visible spectrum on each curve is recorded. Thus, for any given pigment, 144 separate recordings are made—16 on each of nine letdown concentrations. These data are referred to as pigment data. This information is entered into the computer memory for storage or as needed depending upon the program being used. Certain noncolorimetric data on each pigment —chemical resistance, durability characteristics, cost, etc.—are also entered into the computer memory. Inclusion of this latter information equips the computer to make more complete decisions. If, in a given situation, pigments that will match the desired color are lacking in the noncolorimetric characteristics required, the computer will reject them in favor of pigments that meet all specifications.

Standards

One persistent difficulty in color matching in the paint industry stems from the lack of proper color standards. This creates problems in visual matching, and they are complicated further when matching is done instrumentally. If the colors in paint films were permanent, some but not all of the difficulty would exist. The standards would still be affected by scratches, finger marks, and soil. There are certain paint formulations with superior resistance to these hazards and in which the color is comparatively stable. It is easier to maintain standards in this type of finish. It should not be concluded that a finish lacking the characteristics of a good paint standard is not a satisfactory paint. A standard made from an exterior house paint, for example, might have poor color retention when stored in the dark. The film might be relatively soft, easily scratched, and show finger marks when handled, yet this same material applied to a house will give years of satisfactory service.

To obtain better color retention and handling characteristics, it is fairly common to make color standards in a quality other than the material itself (5). This technique was explored by the Sherwin-Williams Co. in 1950, and air drying acrylic color standards were developed for house paints. More recently, baking acrylics are being used, and this procedure is also followed in preparing standards for other paint products. When standards are made in a quality different from that for which they will be the control, the same pigmentation must be used so the standard and the batch will not be metameric.

While standards made with acrylic materials have better color retention and mar resistance, they do not in themselves completely solve the problem of color drift. This has brought about a somewhat novel approach to the storage of standards.

Most chemical reactions cease at very low temperatures. Since color change in a paint film is a chemical reaction, low temperature storage of standards should greatly reduce or completely inhibit color drift. It was found that storage at $-10°F$ accomplished this, and at Sherwin-Williams all master, secondary, and working standards are now stored in domestic type frost-free freezers (3). Spectrophotometric data obtained on all standards prior to storage serve as a check on color stability. If a given standard is used for a length of time for visual or instrumental color matching, it becomes finger marked, scratched, and soiled. This, of course, affects its color, and it becomes unreliable as a standard. The solution is to have "expendable standards."

Three classifications of standards are desirable: (1) master, (2) secondary, (3) working. The master standard should be used only to check the accuracy of instrument readings and the secondary standard but not to check production runs, or it will soon deteriorate to the point where it is no longer valid. The secondary standards are used for instrumental and visual checks for batches in process. When a batch matches the secondary standard instrumentally or visually, it shall be considered satisfactory by both the manufacturer and customer. Working standards are those which can be used by shaders or testers as "color guides" for initial shading of the batch. When the batch approaches the standard for color, the secondary standards are used. Inasmuch as they are only guides for color, they do not have to be a perfect match to the secondary standards. The working standards are expendable. When they are no longer satisfactory for color, they are replaced.

Computer Color Formulation

Many types of computer-controlled color formulation programs are used in the paint industry. While they may differ considerably, they have at least one thing in common: they all utilize the Kubella-Munk theory (1). Described below is one system for arriving at the proper selection of pigments and concentrations to match a given sample. A flow chart of the procedure is shown in Figure 2.

For a new development, the paint formulator is given a standard to match for color and other characteristics. He may or may not need a spectral match to the standard. If that is a requirement, the formulator is limited to using those pigments that are in the standard. In any event, his starting point is a spectrophotometric curve of the standard. This is obtained from a continuous recording instrument such as the General Electric recording spectrophotometer or an abridged spectrophotometer such as the Color-Eye.

Every color produces a peculiar spectrophotometric curve. Each pigment in the color contributes its own characteristics. By selecting

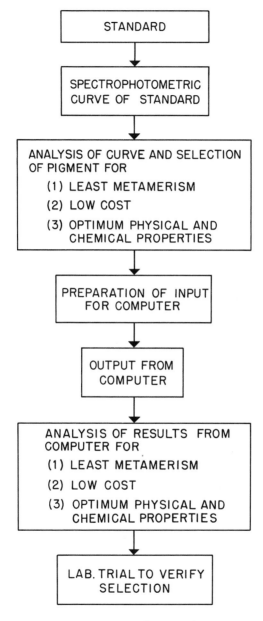

Figure 2. Computer color formulation flow diagram

those individual pigments whose curves coincide with these areas throughout the spectrum of the unknown standard, one can tentatively identify the pigmentation of this standard. If a least-cost match is desired, the least expensive pigments which might match the standard are chosen for computer input. If special physical and chemical properties such as light fastness and alkali resistance are needed in the formulation, pigments satisfying these restrictions are selected. Reflectance data for the standard and the selected pigments are assembled for computer input. These data consist of 16 reflectance points obtained at 20-nm intervals from 400 to 700 nm across each curve. Punched in tape, this information and other pertinent data are entered into the General Electric time sharing system in the following specific order:

(1) Standard.

(2) Starting point (usually white).

(3) Number of pigments selected.

(4) Material from which pigment data were generated.

(5) Individual pigments, concentration, and cost.

The program combines the data on three pigments and white and seeks to match the standard. The process is repeated until all combinations have been tried, and each solution is printed out. If all the pigment quantities for a given solution are positive, the color can be matched with that combination. If any one of the pigment quantities is negative, the color cannot be matched with that combination.

Output consists of the following 10 items for each solution:

(1) Identification heading for standard colors.

(2) Pigments and amounts.

(3) MI: metamerism index.

(4) SS: sum of the squared difference at each of the 16 wavelengths between the standard curve and the predicted curve.

(5) Cost per pound.

(6) Standard's tristimulus values calculated from its 16 reflectance points.

(7) Present ratios: ratios of the tristimulus values for the sample to those of the standard.

(8) Predicted ratios: ratios of the pigment solution to those of the standard.

(9) Differences between standard curve and predicted curve.

(10) Number of iterations required to match the standard color with ratios of 100.0, 100.0, 100.0 ± 0.1.

A spectral solution is indicated by a low MI (< 0.5) and a low SS (< 5.0). Experience has shown these criteria work well. A least-cost solution is shown by the combination of pigments with the lowest cost per pound. Other solutions shown might satisfy the physical and chemical requirements of the formulation sought. An example of a pigment combination that is a spectral match, with both the MI and the SS low, is shown in Figure 3. A combination of pigments that produces a colorimetric match that is highly metameric to the standard is shown in Figure 4.

```
      PIGMENT              CONC

      705500•              2•083

      771360•               •025

      828000•               •574
```

MI =   •2049

SS =   3•1501

CØST PER LB• =   •2832

STD   22•888   23•6193   30•3744

```
PRESENT RATIØS    377•6756    376•6296    324•4262
PREDICT RATIØS     99•9998     99•9998     99•9998
```

1•6 •0 -•1 •0 •1 •0 •1 -•0 -•0 -•1 -•1 •1 •2 •3 •3 •5

IT =   6

Figure 3.   *Output from color formulation program (spectral match)*

Once a solution is obtained, the pigments are ground out, and the laboratory grind is shaded to the standard. This becomes the standard for the production department to match, thus avoiding unwanted metamerism on the production floor. Linear programming, which requires less color knowledge on the part of the formulator, can also be used. This permits one or more parameters to be optimized. Generally, least metamerism and least cost are the parameters optimized. By setting the reflectance data up in a linear program matrix from a given universe of pigments, the matrix can be solved for either least metamerism or least cost.

Production Color Matching

Once a satisfactory formula has been developed, it becomes the responsibility of the production department to produce the material as quickly and efficiently as possible. On any manufacturing foreman's list of production bottlenecks, the subject of color is certain to rank highly. The reason is not difficult to find. A large percentage of production color matching is still done visually by a highly skilled worker classified as a shader or tinter. It is his responsibility to decide which colorants—and the amount of each—are needed to bring a factory batch within color tolerance limits. He must do this with speed and efficiency whether the batch is 50 or 6000 gallons. It takes many years of experience to develop the necessary "know-how" to be an efficient shader. He is considered a key man in the production department of a paint company because of his highly specialized skill.

```
      PIGMENT            CØNC

      771360.            1.297

      843400.            8.815

      828000.            2.783


MI =        3.7415


SS=        667.5029


CØST PER LB.  =         .3036


STD        22.888        23.6193        30.3744


PRESENT RATIØS        377.6756        376.6296        324.4262
PREDICT RATIØS        100.0002        100.0003        100.0001


   22.9-2.7-1.0  .7  .9  1.3  1.5  .5-1.4-1.8  -.5  .7  3.4  6.0  6.1  6.2

I T=        6
```

Figure 4.   Output from color formulation program

Many steps have been taken over the years to help him in his task. Among them has been development of a standard light source for color matching. This gives the shader at least one constant among the many variables to which his visual judgment is subjected. The light source is described in ASTM Method D 1729-64T, Method of Test for "Visual Evaluation of Color Difference of Opaque Materials," and in ISCC, Problem 21, "Visual Evaluation of Small Color Differences." Even with such standardized procedures, shading by the visual method remains an art. The shader's efficiency depends to a large extent on his experience and his emotional and mental attitude at the time the batch is being shaded. Sometimes he can reach the desired color in two attempts; at other times he might require five or six. Therefore, while he is working on the color, production control has been lost, and it is impossible to predict accurately when the batch will be satisfactory for color.

Production Color Matching by Computer

The older, hit-or-miss methods of production color matching are now being challenged by more scientific approaches to the problem. These are made possible by using the Kubelka-Munk theory that predicts the necessary color pigment mixtures, color measuring instruments that reduce the sensation of seeing color to numbers, and high speed computers that handle the complex mathematical calculations. As in color formulation, there are many programs for production color matching, each having advantages and disadvantages. Here again, good data and procedures are more important than any specific program. Like color formulation, they all use some form of the Kubelka-Munk theory.

The way in which these elements may be combined is illustrated in the following program used to achieve a production color match. This program produces accurate results because it utilizes base data to match the standard—*i.e.*, a 1% addition of each base color that will be used to shade the batch is added to a portion of the unshaded batch. A spectrophotometric curve is run on the standard, and the reflectance values at 16 equidistant points across the visible spectrum are recorded. Similar information is secured on the batch being shaded, on 1% additions in the batch of the three base colors selected for use in shading. This must be done only once for each formula since the data can be used every time the batch is made. The data can be obtained from a laboratory batch or a factory batch. The weight per gallon and the size of the batch are also recorded.

Figure 5 shows both the form in which this information is fed into the General Electric Time Sharing System and the computer solution to the problem.

Input:	Lines 1001–2	16 points of the standard
	Lines 1003–4	16 points of the material to which the bases were added
	Lines 1005–6–7	16 points of the 1% letdown of base 1
	Lines 1008–9–10	16 points of the 1% letdown of base 2
	Lines 1001–12–13	16 points of the 1% letdown of base 3
	Lines 1014–15	16 points of batch
	Line 1016	Weight per gallon and size of batch
Output:	Lines 1017–18–19	Concentration of base to the batch, amount of base needed for 100 gallons, and amount needed for batch

Figure 6 shows the output when the same problem is fed into an IBM 1130 computer. In this case the data on the standard, bases, etc. are stored in the computer for recall as needed, so only the data on the ratios of the tristimulus values of the batch to the standard, the batch name, and the size of the batch need be entered. As is usually the case

SW TIME SHARE

GE TIME-SHARING SERVICE

ØN AT 13:51   CK FRI 08/30/68

USER NUMBER--K10000
SYSTEM--BAS
NEW ØR ØLD--ØLD
ØLD FILE NAME--BPS10*
WAIT.

FILE SIZE LIMIT

READY.

TAPE
READY

```
1000 DATA SPECIAL BLUE ENAMEL++++++++++++++++++++0

1001 DATA 44.3,47.5,51.9,57.9,62.6,63.0,61.3,57.9
1002 DATA 52.2,44.0,34.1,28.2,26.5,27.1,30.1,32.7
1003 DATA 33.2,48.7,54.7,62.1,68.3,69.4,67.4,63.1
1004 DATA 56.3,47.6,37.9,31.6,29.2,28.5,30.5,32.3
1005 DATA 790851,.01
1006 DATA 28.0,39.3,45.8,55.3,64.3,66.3,63.3,57.5
1007 DATA 48.6,38.4,27.9,21.7,19.5,19.0,20.9,22.6
1008 DATA 770250,.01
1009 DATA 32.6,47.8,53.9,61.4,66.9,66.6,62.0,54.0
1010 DATA 43.8,35.7,29.5,25.7,24.9,25.1,26.2,27.0
1011 DATA 705590,.01
1012 DATA 29.6,40.3,43.0,45.5,46.8,46.4,45.1,43.4
1013 DATA 40.5,36.4,30.8,26.6,24.8,24.2,25.5,26.5
1014 DATA 33.2,47.6,37.9,31.6,29.2,28.5,30.5,32.3
1015 DATA 56.3,47.6,37.9,31.6,29.2,28.5,30.5,32.3
1016 DATA 0,10.57,2200,100,100,100
```

RUN

BPS10*   13:54   CK FRI 08/30/68

BASE	CØNC	LBS/100 GALS	LBS/BATCH
790851	9.48169 E-2	1.00221	22.0487
770250	8.68131 E-2	.917615	20.1875
705590	.129307	1.36678	30.0691
STD	41.2215	49.7495	65.5392
PRESENT RATIØS	108.477	109.092	106.621
PREDICT RATIØS	100.006	100.008	100.002

Figure 5. GE computer input and output for production color matching

REX   SPECIAL BLUE ENAMEL

SIZE   2200

RATIOS   108.5   109.1   106.6

BASE	CONC	LBS/100 GALS	LBS/BATCH
790851	.095	1.00	22.05
770250	.087	.920	20.19
705590	.129	1.37	30.07
STD	41.22	49.75	65.54
PRESENT RATIOS 108.48		109.1	106.6
PREDICT RATIOS 100.01		100.01	100.0

Figure 6.   IBM input and output for production color matching

when a new process is implemented, production shading by computer has forced a tightening of production procedures and testing methods. Shading bases must be controlled for tinting strength and weighed accurately into the batch. The sample paint-out must be truly representative of the batch. There can be no substitution of pigments or shading bases.

Tolerances

Since it is rarely economically feasible to match color standards perfectly in production, the limits of permissible color deviation should be included in every specification. This deviation, or tolerance, must be small enough to ensure that the color is satisfactory, yet it must be broad enough to permit economical manufacture of the product. At present in the paint industry, there are three methods for determining whether or not a production color is within the tolerance permitted: visual examination, instrumentation, and a combination of the two.

Visual Examination

No instrument can perceive small color differences as quickly and accurately as the human eye. However, visual observers have poor color memory. To detect small color differences, they must view samples side by side. Standard conditions for viewing increase the reliability of visual color judgments. However, even under the best conditions, an observer or group of observers, will be inconsistent in color judgment because individual reactions to color are themselves inconsistent. An all too common system of color tolerance is to state that the batch must be a "good visual match to the standard." In effect, this is no tolerance at all since it leaves everything to personal opinion. Such opinion is influenced by many extraneous factors, including the end use of the product. Certainly a good match in a floor paint would not be considered a good match in a pre-finished siding finish. Yet, with no other guideline than the admonition to provide a "good" match, an observer might interpret the limits too closely or too broadly.

In view of this, it is advisable to set limits related to the three dimensions of color: hue, chroma, and lightness (or value). Sometimes limits for only one or two of the dimensions are given. An example is the Federal Highway Marking Specification set up in 1939 and still used for yellow traffic marking paint. This tolerance specifies the hue difference in terms of green and red variations from the standard. No limits are set for saturation or lightness, so these dimensions are a matter for personal opinion or arbitration. If limits were set on these attributes of color too, the observer would have a much more complete idea of what is required.

Instrumentation

If colorimeters can accurately determine numerical values for colors and the colors being compared are even slightly different, the difference in the numbers should describe how far apart the colors are. Unfortunately, this is not always true when the data are drawn from the three sets of values usually obtained from colorimeters (11). The difficulty stems from the fact that the numerical differences between pairs of different colors do not parallel in magnitude visual differences on the same samples. To correct this situation, the values must be converted in some manner to take into consideration the three dimensions of color and their relationship to each other. A tolerance can be established in two broad categories —numerical and graphical. In either case, data must be obtained from some type of colorimeter. It is essential that numerical tolerances be written in terms of the data obtained (7). For example, if color-eye data are supplied expressing values in terms of X, Y and Z, a system that utilizes data in this form will be most effective. Although formulas are available to convert data from one form to another, accuracy is frequently sacrificed in the process.

There are several accepted methods for determining color difference in terms of numerical values. None of them is perfect, but when used with certain precautions they are reliable and superior to visual methods. One widely used formula for calculating color difference is usually referred to as NBS units. This system expresses color difference from the coordinates L, a and b, with L = lightness, $+a$ = red, $-a$ = green, $+b$ = yellow, and $-b$ = blue. The formula is as follows:

$$\Delta E \sqrt{\Delta L^2 + \Delta a^2 + \Delta b^2}$$

ΔL, Δa, and Δb are the differences of the coordinates between the batch and the standard. Data in this form are readily obtained from the Hunter-lab color difference meter and the Gardner color difference meter and from the Color-Master when a set of charts is used. The popularity of this formula for computing color difference arises from the simplicity of the calculations involved and the fact that many instruments now in use provide data in terms of L, a, and b. This convenience alone would not justify the use of the formula; it must also be reliable, which it is. However, like any one-number system for describing color difference, it has limitations because it reveals only total color difference and not the direction of the difference.

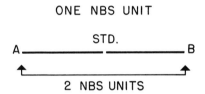

ONE NBS UNIT

*Figure 7. Simple diagram show-
ing possible variation of two samples from a standard*

If a numerical system for use in production is to be successful, the direction of the color difference permitted must be made known. This should be agreed upon by the purchaser and the seller because usually the purchaser has a preference even though it is not always expressed. If the direction from the standard is agreed upon, then the tolerance system is truly usable. To illustrate, assume a specification permits a tolerance of 1 NBS unit. What is implied is that the color may differ from the standard by 1 NBS unit in all directions, but often this is not what is meant. Figure 7 is an oversimplified diagram showing this. Sample A could be 1 NBS unit away from the standard but on the red side of the standard. Sample B, also 1 NBS unit away from the standard, is on the green side. Both samples meet the required tolerance, but compared with one another they are a total of 2 NBS units apart. The purchaser may not permit one sample on the red side and the other on the green side since they would show too large a visible difference.

In this connection it may be useful to point out the relationship between NBS units and the color differences the eye can detect. A just perceptible difference would be about 0.3 NBS unit. This does not mean that an acceptable match has to be below 0.3 NBS unit variation because match acceptability varies with products. However, it does suggest that acceptable matches can range from 0.3 NBS unit upwards, depending on how close a match is desired. In the hypothetical case illustrated by Figure 7, the samples probably would be more acceptable if they were all on the red side or all on the green side since they would then have the same hue.

Instruments excel in this type of control because limits can be put on the numerical values obtained from them to keep the samples in the same hue area in color space. Assume the tolerance for a yellow standard is 1 NBS unit, but a further restriction is that the batch must have a $+a$ value. Figure 8 shows that all the samples are now on the red side of the standard. To obtain an even more sophisticated tolerance, saturation can be controlled by requiring that the samples not be on the blue side of the standard because as blue is added to a yellow, the latter becomes grayer. This could be accomplished by requiring that all the b values must be zero or on the plus side. If the specification read that samples could have only $+a$ and $+b$, they would all be in the red area and appear clean to the standard.

ONE NBS UNIT RESTRICTED
$\triangle a$ MUST BE PLUS (RED)

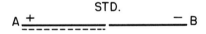

Figure 8.   Simple diagram of restricted tolerance

The specification now leaves only one variable unaccounted for— L or lightness. This can be controlled by stipulating whether the sample can be either lighter or darker than the standard. With this restriction, the specification reads:

We must have a total color difference of not more than 1 NBS unit, Δa must be zero or plus, Δb must be zero or plus, ΔL must be equal to or larger than the standard.

With this type of tolerance, there is no question about what the manufacturer is supposed to produce.

Another equation for computing color difference is the MacAdam equation. From their study of various color difference equations, the New York Society for Paint Technology concluded that this equation was superior to other color difference equations and that it was the most reliable to use in color difference calculations. A color difference of 1 MacAdam unit is a just noticeable difference.

The formula for computing MacAdam tolerance is:

$$\Delta E = 1/K \left(\overline{\Delta x}^2 g_{11} + \Delta x\, \Delta y\, 2g_{12} + \overline{\Delta y}^2 g_{22} + \overline{G\Delta Y}^2 \right)^{\frac{1}{2}}$$

where
$$\Delta E = \text{Units of MacAdam color difference}$$
$$g_{11}, g_{12}, g_{22} = \text{Constants describing the MacAdam ellipse}$$
$$K = \text{Corrects ellipse size for lightness}$$
$$G = \text{Adds for lightness difference}$$
$$\Delta x, \Delta y = \text{Chromaticity coordinate difference between two samples}$$
$$\Delta Y = Y \text{ value difference between two samples}$$

Unfortunately, this is an extremely complicated equation requiring difficult and lengthy computation. As it stands, it is impractical for use in production color control of large numbers of samples. However, through the use of a series of charts developed initially by Davidson and Hanlon and later improved upon by Simon and Goodman (*10*), the necessary calculations can be speeded. A similar set of charts developed by R. S. Foster eliminates some of the calculations entirely (*2*).

To eliminate more of the lengthy calculations, the Sherwin-Williams Co. has developed a series of ellipses for each color being controlled. Use of such ellipses is not new. Lawrence Rudick and George Ingle in 1952 reported their use for establishing color tolerances for plastics (*9*). They pointed out that plots showing three views of concentric portions of the color solid are necessary to represent the three dimensions of color. They set tolerances for each color, and these were plotted concentrically with MacAdam ellipses around the standard point. The size of the solid ellipsoid was fixed by the data from the accumulated physical limit specifications.

Figure 9 shows that it is first necessary to compute the chromaticity coordinates *x* and *y*. Once these are known, the plots can then be made on the three charts. The size of the ellipses are predetermined in terms of MacAdam units. If a sample plots within all three ellipses, it is said to be satisfactory for color. This method requires considerable calculation when the Color-Eye is used as the measuring instrument. The *X*, *Y*, and *Z* values have to be converted to CIE *X*, *Y*, and *Z* values, and those, in turn, have to be converted to *x*, *y*, and *Y*. Although this can be done with charts and a slide rule or desk calculator, it is time consuming and not very pratical when many production samples must be checked.

To overcome this difficulty, a method has been developed in which the coordinates of the ellipses are stated in terms of Color-Eye ratios. The MacAdam ellipses, which use the coordinates *x*, *y*, and *Y* are converted to

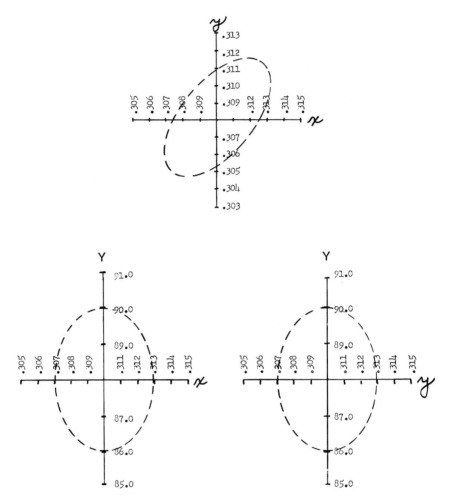

Figure 9.   Inspection tolerance ellipsoids for white plastic

the X, Y, and Z ratio coordinates and projected on three planes. This enables the operator to use the data obtained from the color-eye on the
ellipses (Figure 10) to determine without calculation whether the sample
is within the tolerance. This procedure is essentially a rapid go–no go system. Its single drawback is that one sample can be on the red side of
the standard by 1 MacAdam unit and another can be on the green side
by 1 unit. As a result, the samples are actually 2 units apart when
compared.

Warping the true MacAdam ellipses (Figure 11) results in a tolerance more acceptable by visual comparison. This tolerance controls
which side of the standard the sample should be on by stating that X

must be equal to or higher than Y and Z and that Y must be equal to or higher than Z. Additional information added to the ellipse indicates the pigments needed to obtain ratios that will plot within the tolerance and thus be satisfactory for color. There are times when the direction of the variation from the standard does not have to be specified. This occurs when the sample approaches a perfect match to the standard. Experience

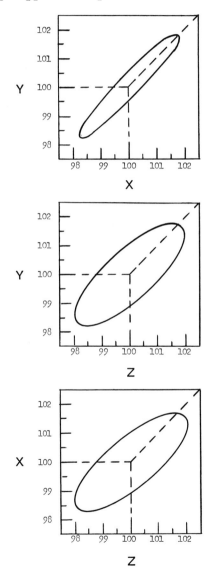

Figure 10.   Direct reading tolerance chart from color-eye ratios (white enamel, 1.5 ΔE)

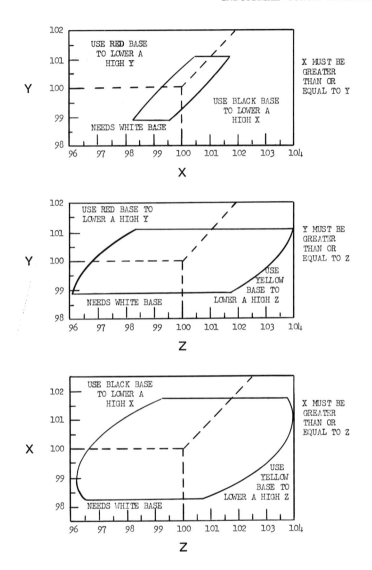

*Figure 11.   Restricted direct reading tolerance chart from
color-eye ratios (yellow enamel, 2.0 ΔE)*

indicates that at 0.25 or less of the total tolerance, the direction from the
standard need not be specified. If, for example, the tolerance were 2
MacAdam units, anything within 0.5 MacAdam unit would not have to
be restricted. Tolerance charts representing this idea are shown in Figure
12. A sample that plots within the small areas of all three ellipses can vary
in any direction from the standard.

Establishing Limits

In establishing a color tolerance, customer acceptability must be used as a basis. Hence, the first step in accumulating physical limit specimens that represent as complete a range of customer acceptability as possible. The specimens should be in all directions colorimetrically from the standard. However, this may not always be possible because the customer's acceptability may be in one direction from the standard. It is most

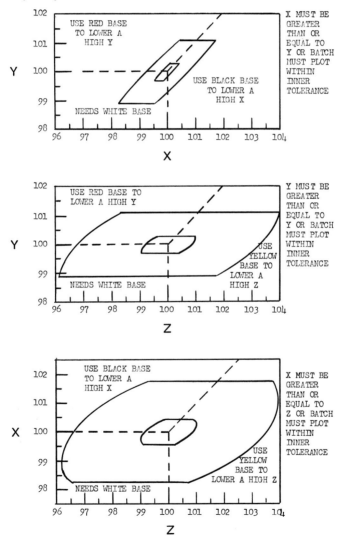

Figure 12. Restricted direct reading tolerance charts from color-eye ratios with unrestricted centers (yellow enamel, 2.0 ΔE)

important that all samples be spectrally similar to the standard, and care should be exercised to avoid metamerism. Since actual production samples will show chromaticity and reflectance variation from the standard, the difference must be characteristic in three dimensions.

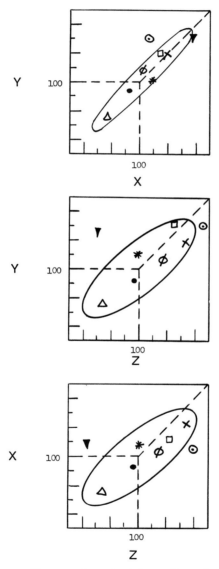

Figure 13. MacAdam ellipsoids to determine customer acceptance (2 MacAdam units). All samples plotting within ellipsoid were acceptable to customer.

Another way to determine limits is to record the color difference values of the color the purchaser accepts and rejects. Tolerance can also be established by preparing ellipses whose limits are what the customer will probably accept (Figure 13). If the customer is rejecting materials that plot within the tolerance, the tolerance must be narrowed so it rejects those samples the customer rejects. Care must be taken not to include exceptional cases. Until the tolerances are satisfactory to all concerned, they must of necessity be negotiable. The customer has the right to ask for tighter tolerances if they are realistic. The supplier can suggest that the tolerances be broadened if compliance seriously hinders production. It must be understood that there are limitations on the accuracy of instruments, and the instrument's capability must be taken into account when tolerances are established.

Frequently tolerances are set up by merely specifying equal plus and minus values from the dial readings of the colorimeter. An example of this type of tolerance would be equal plus and minus values of ΔL, Δa, and Δb as the limits. The simplicity of setting up this type of tolerance is offset by the complications that result from its use. Such a tolerance is often much more stringent than necessary. To illustrate, assume a tolerance for a green enamel with a plus or minus ΔL, Δa, Δb of 0.5 NBS unit. If a sample deviated 0.5 unit from the standard on the green side, the batch would be acceptable because it would be within the tolerance and would look satisfactory. However, if the sample deviated 0.5 unit in the red, it might be rejected because 0.5 unit would be too much variation of red in a green. Since the sample would be within the ± 0.5 unit tolerance but would not have a satisfactory appearance, the customer might want to reduce the total tolerance to something like 0.25 unit. This could present problems. It might be better to reduce only that part of the tolerance which controls the red. Then the redesigned tolerance would permit variation of 0.5 unit on the green side but only 0.25 unit on the red side of the standard. This will require different limits for ΔL, Δa, and Δb, depending on what color is being considered. There is a tendency when numerical tolerances are established to make them more restrictive than the previous visual tolerances. This slows production and discourages the use of instruments for color control.

Conclusion

In the beginning, paint making by its very nature was an art. Its beginning was so simple that it is hard to determine when it actually began. As any manufacturing process progresses, it gradually changes from an art to a science, and the paint industry is no exception. During this evolution there is a shift from human judgment to instrumentation.

One phase at a time has given way to modern techniques. The old stone mills have been replaced by high speed dispersing equipment. Varnish making has passed from the old varnish maker to a modern controlled scientific process. Now color matching is becoming a more scientific operation.

We are certain that with improving techniques, better instruments, and computers, color formulation and production color matching will soon reach the same level as the other phases of paint manufacturing. Colorimetry and high speed computers will soon make the majority of the color decisions in the paint laboratories and factories.

Literature Cited

(1) Allen, Eugene, "Analytical Color Matching," *Offic. Digest, Federation Soc. Paint Technol.* **1967,** 39, 268.
(2) Foster, R. S., "A New Simplified System of Charts for Rapid Color Difference Calculations," *Color Eng.* **Jan.-Feb. 1966,** 17.
(3) Huey, Sam J., "Low Temperature Storage of Color Standard Panels," *Color Eng.* **Sept.-Oct. 1965,** 24.
(4) Johnston, Ruth M., "Spectrophotometry for the Analysis and Description of Color," *Offic. Digest, Federation Soc. Paint Technol.* **1967,** 39, 346.
(5) Johnston, Ruth M., Richards, Thomas D., Rosenthal, Williams, "Preparation and Use of Stable Secondary Standards for Colorimetry," *Color Eng.* **March-April 1968,** p. 34-38.
(6) Lytle, Jack R., Leete, Charles G., "A Digital Computer Technique for Calculation of Dominant Wavelength," *Color Eng.* **Jan.-Feb. 1966,** 27.
(7) Martens, C. R., "Technology of Paints, Varnishes, and Lacquers," Reinhold Publishing Corp., pp. 472-482, 1968.
(8) Orwig, B. R., "Polar Strength and Dispersability of Pigments by the Sherwin-Williams Miniature Sand Mill," *Paint Technol.* **1967,** 39, 14.
(9) Rudick, Lawrence, Ingle, George W., "Control of Small Color Difference in Plastic Manufacturing," *ASTM Symp. Color Difference Specifications,* **1952,** pp. 10.
(10) Simon, R. T., Goodwin, W. J., "Rapid Graphical Computation of Small Color Difference," *Am. Dyestuff Reptr.* **1958,** 47, 102.
(11) "So You Want to Set Color Tolerances," *Offic. Digest, Federation Soc. Paint Technol.* **1967,** 39, 346.

RECEIVED June 6, 1969.

INDEX

INDEX